THE ISLAMIC TRILOGY
VOLUME 1

MOHAMMED AND THE UNBELIEVERS

A POLITICAL LIFE

THE ISLAMIC TRILOGY SERIES

THE ISLAMIC TRILOGY

VOLUME 1

MOHAMMED AND THE UNBELIEVERS

A POLITICAL LIFE

CENTER FOR THE STUDY
OF POLITICAL ISLAM

CSPI PUBLISHING

THE ISLAMIC TRILOGY
VOLUME 1

MOHAMMED AND THE UNBELIEVERS

A POLITICAL LIFE

COPYRIGHT © 2006 CSPI, LLC

ISBN 0-9785528-9-X
ISBN13 978-0-9785528-9-3

V5.22.06

PUBLISHED BY CSPI, LLC
WWW.CSPIPUBLISHING.COM

PRINTED IN THE USA

TABLE OF CONTENTS

THE CSPI MAXIM

Islam is a political system, a culture, and a religion based upon the Koran, Sira, and Hadith. To understand Islam, know the Trilogy.

PURPOSE

The Center for the Study of Political Islam is dedicated to:
- *Making the political doctrine of the Koran, Sira, and Hadith (the Trilogy) available to the world.*
- *Establishing authoritative/verifiable fact-based knowledge—statements that can be confirmed by the use of reference numbers.*
- *Integrating knowledge—using primary sources to give the complete picture of Islam's political doctrine.*

OVERVIEW

Islam is a political system, a culture, and a religion. The religion of Islam is what a Muslim does to go to Paradise and avoid Hell. Political Islam determines the treatment of unbelievers and the governance of Muslims. The internal politics of Islam are not of interest here.

The chief features of the religion are charity to other Muslims, prayer to Allah, fasting during the month of Ramadan, pilgrimage to Mecca, and declaring that Mohammed is the prophet of the only god, Allah. The religion of Islam is important to Muslims, but the politics affect every non-Muslim.

Islam has a complete legal code, the Sharia. The foundation of Islam's legal and political system is clearly laid out in three texts—the Koran, the Sira, and the Hadith—the Islamic Trilogy. Every book of the Trilogy is both religious and political. More than half of the Koran focuses on the unbelievers. About three-quarters of the Sira (life of Mohammed) is political. The Hadith is filled with political statements and examples. Islam is a fully developed political system and the oldest form of politics active today.

The fundamental principle of Islam is that its politics are sacred, perfect, eternal, and universal. All other political systems are man-made and must be replaced by Islamic law.

Islam's success comes primarily from its politics. In thirteen years as a spiritual leader, Mohammed converted 150 people to his religion. When he became a political leader and warrior, Islam exploded, and Mohammed became king of Arabia in ten years.

THE GOAL OF THE TRILOGY SERIES

This work is part of a series titled, "The Islamic Trilogy." The volumes correspond to the sacred texts of Islam: Mohammed's biography (known as the Sira), his proverbs and practices (known as the Hadith), and the revelation of Allah (known as the Koran). Until this publication, the Sira and the Hadith were previously available only to scholars.

"The Islamic Trilogy" is designed to clarify the original texts. The barrier to understanding these texts is their scholarly complexity. The Hadith

(Traditions) is found primarily in two collections by Bukhari and Abu Muslim. The total number of stories is about 14,000. They are highly repetitive with as many as twelve subtle versions of the same story. The Sira (Mohammed's biography) is 600 pages in small print filled with Arabic terms. The Koran is obscure and confusing.

The Trilogy makes the Sira available in only 200 pages with nearly every paragraph referenced to the original text. The Hadith is made accessible by choosing those hadiths that refer to unbelievers and omitting the strictly religious hadiths. The Koran is made easy to understand by using modern English. Every verse is included. When Mohammed's life is woven throughout the Koran, the meaning is restored, and it becomes a powerful epic story. Reading the Trilogy makes reading the original texts simple.

ISLAM

Most non-Muslims think Islam is based entirely upon the Koran. Islam is based upon the Koran and the words and deeds of Mohammed. Actually, there is not enough information in the Koran to establish the practice of the religion; the Sira and the Hadith are necessary. The Koran repeats more than thirty times that a Muslim is to obey Mohammed in word and deed, and more than forty times it condemns those who do not. In order to know what those words and deeds are, one must read the biography (Sira) and proverbs and practices (Hadith) of Mohammed. How did Mohammed eat dates? Tie his shoes? Practice sex? Pray? Go to war? Brush his teeth? Urinate? Drink a glass of water? There is no other person in history about whom we know such small, personal details. Still, all of these details are not just about Mohammed; they are directions on how to be the ideal Muslim.

The Koran declares that it is the word of Allah, the only god, and says that Allah is pleased when the world imitates Mohammed in every aspect of his life, including religion. The daily actions of a Muslim are far more governed by the Hadith and the Sira than the Koran. When Muslims say they are the "believers" they mean that they believe in Mohammed and the Koran.

A SACRED TEXT

What you are about to read is not merely a story or a history or a biography but a sacred text. Muslims believe that Mohammed's attitude, actions, and words are the ideal pattern of human behavior for all times and all peoples. The smallest detail of his life teaches pure Islam. It is for that reason that each chapter starts with a verse from the Koran that commands all Muslims to imitate Mohammed in every detail of his words and deeds. Mohammed's life defines Islam.

It is hard for a non-Muslim to grasp the profound reverence and awe that Muslims feel for Mohammed. The religion is Islam, but the practice is Mohammedan (being a Mohammedan no more means worshiping Mohammed than being a Confucian means worshiping Confucius).

A POLITICAL TEXT

The Sira is a detailed manual that lays out the complete strategy of political Islam and jihad. Much of the Sira is about how Mohammed dealt with those people who disagreed with him. Violent political action with a religious motivation was taken against non-Muslims. Under Islam, their only political freedom was to submit.

ABOUT THIS BOOK

The primary sources of all biographical material on Mohammed are Ishaq's *Sirat Rasul Allah* (*Life of the Prophet of Allah*, usually called the Sira) and Al Tabari's *History of Prophets and Kings*. Tabari's history consists of thirty-nine volumes, four of which are about Mohammed's life. It also covers the expansion of Islam as it conquered the world over the centuries. These works date back to about 800 AD, nearly two hundred years after the death of Mohammed.

Another excellent biography used as a resource here is Sir William Muir's *Life of Mohammed*, written in 1923. Its language is late nineteenth-century English, but it is very factual and an easy read.

Most of the following content is a condensed version of Ishaq's Sira. Occasional quotes appear from the Koran and Hadith as well. The most widely accepted hadiths by Muslim scholars are those by Al Bukhari and Abu Muslim; the source text is indicated in each instance. When the source text is not indicated, remarks are those of the contributing scholars.

Ishaq's original account is disjointed. To solve this problem, this work rearranges the text as necessary, with a two-fold purpose of clarity and faithfulness to the original.

This work's viewpoint is not neutral. It is written from the standpoint of the non-Muslim. Islam divides the world into two portions:

dar al Islam, the land of submission, and

dar al harb, the land of war.

The Center for the Study of Political Islam, believing there is a sufficient number of works from the land of submission, the victors, has published *Mohammed and the Unbelievers* from the land of war, the view of the victims.

TECHNICAL NOTES

Ishaq's Sira contains many stories of miracles; yet it also says Mohammed refused to perform miracles. The Koran's text is older than the Sira and says that Mohammed was a messenger who did no miracles, so the miracles have been omitted from this account to resolve the inconsistency.

Variant spellings of Mohammed (Muhammad), Koran (Quran), and other Arabic words are used today and the spellings used within were chosen merely for consistency's sake.

Text in parentheses is original to the source documents; text in brackets was inserted by the editors.

The story of Islam and Mohammed happened in an isolated part of the world, Arabia. There are no supporting documents from any other culture about a single event in Mohammed's life. Only after Mohammed's death and the Islamic invasion of the rest of the world are there any independent sources of Islamic history.

THE REFERENCE SYSTEM

Both the Ishaq and Al Tabari texts use a system of margin notes referring to the original page in the Arabic text. Examples of this system:

I 123 is a reference to Ishaq's Sira, margin note 123.

T123 is a reference to *The History of al Tabari*, State University of New York Press, margin note 123.

Other references within this work:

M123 is a page reference to W. Muir, *The Life of Mohammed*, AMS Press, 1975.

2:123 is a reference to the Koran, chapter 2, verse 123.

B1,3,4 is a reference to *Sahih Bukhari*, volume 1, book 3, number 4.

M012, 1234 is a reference to *Sahih Muslim*, book 12, number 1234.

The Center for the Study of Political Islam avers the authenticity and accuracy of this series. Nevertheless, it counsels the thoughtful and contemplative reader to regard it merely as a helpful appendix for examining the original text itself.

IN THE BEGINNING

CHAPTER 1

3:32 Say: Obey Allah and His messenger, but if they reject it,
then truly, Allah does not love those who reject the faith.

TO THE READER

It is important to read the overview on page vii. This is not an ordinary story and you must understand its context.

THE LIFE OF THE PROPHET OF ALLAH

Fourteen hundred years ago in Arabia, there was an orphan who became the first king of Arabia. His name, Mohammed, would become one of the most common names in the world. He was to create a kingdom that would dwarf the Roman Empire. According to the god of the Arabs, he was the ideal pattern for all men, and he would make the god of the Arabs the god of all. The smallest detail of his behavior would set the pattern of life for billions.

Mohammed's father was called Abdullah, meaning "slave of Allah." There were many gods in Arabia at that time. Allah, a moon god, was the tribal god of the Quraysh, the ruling clan of Mecca. Allah was a high god of the many gods worshipped in the town of Mecca.

Mohammed was still in his mother's womb when his father died, and when he was five his mother died. His grandfather raised Mohammed and then he was orphaned for the third time when his grandfather died. His uncle, Abu Talib, then took him in. All were of the Quraysh tribe. These brief facts are about all of the history known about Mohammed's early childhood.

MOHAMMED'S TRIBE—THE QURAYSH

When Mohammed was born, there was no nation of Arabia, no Arabian king, and no political unity. Society was tribal in nature; a person was not an individual so much as a member of a tribe. Blood relations were everything, and when people met the first question was, "What are your tribe and your lineage?" A person's name provided a clue to his lineage. In

1

fact, without a tribe, an individual was very weak and fair game. Squabbling and fighting among clans were common and ruled by blood laws, which were the laws of retaliation and "an eye for an eye and a tooth for a tooth." Under certain circumstances blood money could be paid to the surviving kin.

The Quraysh tribe came to Mecca five generations before Mohammed under the leadership of Qusayy, who established the rituals of worship in Mecca. The Quraysh became the priestly tribe of Mecca, similar to the Levi or Cohen of the Jews, and were the nobility of the town holding the ceremonial offices. In addition, the Quraysh were traders and businessmen, blending religion and business when pilgrims came to town for religious services. Mohammed's clan was the Hashim clan, which is still active in politics today.

MECCA AS A RELIGIOUS CENTER

Mecca in Mohammed's day was very small, about a quarter mile by an eighth of a mile, and it was in an area of Arabia called the Hijaz. The climate of Mecca is dry, very dry, but when a heavy rain comes it causes huge runoffs so that Mecca will actually flood for a brief time.

There was a stone building in Mecca in the shape of a cube called the *Kabah* that was a religious site containing images of several tribal gods. There were at least six other square stone houses called Kabahs in other towns in Arabia; however, the legend about the Kabah in Mecca was that Abraham, the patriarch of the Jews, had built it. The Kabah was used for religious rituals and served as a community center. Rituals established by Qusayy included prostrations (bowing down to the earth), ritual prayers, circling the Kabah while praying, and drinking from the well called Zam Zam. Other rituals included throwing stones at pillars that symbolized the devil.

Stones played an important part in the religions of Arabia. The Kabah was made of stone and had the important Black Stone built into one corner. This stone was probably a meteorite as it was a composite of several stones melded together. It was small in size, roughly seven inches in diameter, and was touched only with the right hand and kissed by pilgrims. All of these native rituals were incorporated into Islam.

Each tribe had its gods and the moon god, Allah, seems to have been a male god of the Quraysh. There was not much of an organization of the Arabic gods, unlike the Greek and Roman gods, but children were named after them; for instance, Mohammed's father was named after Allah, but his brothers were named after other Arabic gods.

MOHAMMED IN MECCA

EARLY LIFE

CHAPTER 2

*3:131 Obey Allah and His messenger so
that you may receive mercy.*

I130-136,150I The Sira says that Christians and Jews knew from their scriptures that Mohammed was coming, but these scriptures are unknown to them. Not only the monotheists but many Arab mystics and soothsayers are said to have prophesied the coming of Mohammed. According to the Sira all the religious world was waiting for Mohammed, and he was the fulfillment of all scriptures. Islam gives him a perfect lineage that goes back to Abraham of the Jews and from there back to Adam.

Ishaq's Sira repeatedly claims the conception, pregnancy, birth, and early childhood of Mohammed were all miraculous events, foreshadowing his recognition as prophet of all the world.

Miracles and noble lineage were standard fare for that time. In truth, very little is known of Mohammed's life before he was a grown man. The miracle stories were first recorded two hundred years after his death, and the Koran says he never worked any miracles. The later the history is recorded, the higher the number of miracles it contains. The number of miracles included in a text is a good indicator of when it was written.

CHILDHOOD

I115 Mohammed was eight years old when his grandfather died. He was then raised by Abu Talib, his uncle, who took him on a trading trip to Syria, a very different place from Mecca. Syria was a Christian country that was sophisticated and very much a part of the cosmopolitan culture of the Mediterranean. It was Syrian Christians who gave the Arabs their alphabet. At that time, no book had ever been written in Arabic; only poems and business correspondence had.

MARRIAGE

I120 Mohammed was grown when he was hired by a distant cousin, the wealthy widow Khadija, to act as her trading agent in Syria. Mohammed had a reputation of good character and good business sense. Trading between Mecca and Syria was risky business; it not only took skill to manage a caravan but also to cut the best deal in Syria. Mohammed managed Khadija's affairs well and she turned a good profit.

I120 Khadija was well known among the Quraysh tribe. Sometime after hiring Mohammed as her business agent, she proposed marriage to him. They married and had six children. Their two sons died in childhood and the four daughters lived to adulthood

I121 Khadija had a cousin, Waraqa, who was a Christian. To the north and to the east were the Christian areas of Syria and Turkey, but Christians were rare in Arabia.

REBUILDING THE KABAH

I122 When Mohammed was about thirty-five, the Quraysh religious leaders decided to rebuild the Kabah. It had been rebuilt several times before, but up until then it had never had a roof and some religious objects inside had been stolen. One of the suspected thieves had had his hand cut off and was banished from Mecca.

I123 A roof would make it more secure but would require wood, and wood was in short supply in Mecca. As luck would have it, a Greek ship had been driven ashore near Mecca, which is close to the Red Sea. The timbers of the ship would become the timbers and decking of the Kabah's first roof.

I124 But to put on a roof, it would be necessary to demolish the walls and rebuild them. Since the structure was old and shrouded in mystery, there was some anxiety about the demolition. But one of the Quraysh had the courage to start the task. And with a brief prayer he removed the first stone. Nothing happened and he proceeded to demolish two corners of the stone structure. At the end of the day the Quraysh who were watching decided that if he lived through the night the task had not offended any of the gods of the Kabah.

I125 In the morning they all returned to the task and soon the Kabah had been demolished down to a foundation. Each clan fell to the task of collecting more stones so that the new Kabah would be more substantial for its new roof. Once the new stone structure was completed only one job remained: the ritual task of installing the Black Stone.

I125 Which clan would be privileged to install the most sacred part of the Kabah? The clans argued for days; bloodshed was threatened. They gathered at the grounds to settle the issue. One of the oldest of the Quraysh suggested they let the next man who came through the door decide who of the clans should install the Black Stone. It was agreed and the next man through the door was Mohammed.

1125 Mohammed made a decision that would have pleased Solomon. He had them spread a cloak on the ground and place the Black Stone in the middle of it. Each clan had one of its members grasp the hem of the cloak and lift the stone into place; so the Stone was installed. Another small feud was avoided and, even better, everyone was happy. The Coptic (Egyptian) carpenter took the timbers from the Greek ship and built the first roof for the Kabah.

MONOTHEISM IN ARABIA

1144 The Arabs referred to monotheism as Hanifiya and to those who were monotheists as Hanifs. The strongest strain of monotheism by far was represented by the Jews. After the destruction of Jerusalem by the Romans due to the Zealots' rebellion, Jews dispersed throughout the Middle East, and there was a strong presence of Jews in Arabia. A few local Arabs were Christians, but the type of Christianity in the area of Mecca was unorthodox, with a trinity of God, Jesus, and Mary.

1144 Jews and Christians were "People of the Book." Since there was no book yet published in Arabic, this distinction was a strong one; all the sources of the Arabic religions were found in oral tradition and custom. The Meccans were aware of the Jewish Abrahamic account. Mecca was a long way from Syria where Abraham dwelt, but the Meccans claimed Abraham and Ishmael had built the Kabah in ancient times.

1144 At this time there was a monotheistic pull away from the ancient Arabic tribal religions with their local gods, all with different areas of influence in the world, but there was a tolerance for different religious beliefs. Families in the same clan would include different deities in their worship. These other deities might be brought into the home by marriage outside the clan or tribe.

1144 There were a very few Meccans, including Mohammed's wife's cousin, who became Christians. One of them went to Constantinople and served the emperor. One later became a Muslim (one who has submitted to Allah) and then emigrated to Ethiopia where he converted to Christianity.

1144-149 One monotheist, Zayd, was very interesting. He abandoned all religion and then created his own monotheistic religion. His prayers and rituals were a fusion of Judaic theology and tribal rituals, including prostrations and the use of the Kabah for a prayer focus. He said that Abraham prayed facing the Kabah. He publicly attacked and condemned his tribal members for their beliefs, and he condemned any form of worship of any god except the One-God. He submitted to the unnamed One-God. The One-God was to be feared, heaven was a garden, and infidels would burn in Hell. Much of his poetry used the same language as the Koran. He referenced his worship to the Jewish patriarchs, as they were pure in their worship. Mohammed recognized Zayd as a precursor.

THE FIRST DAYS OF BEING A PROPHET

CHAPTER 3

*4:13 These are the limits set up by Allah. Those who obey
Allah and His Messenger will be led into the Gardens
watered by flowing rivers to live forever. This is the
ultimate reward! But those who disobey Allah and His
Messenger and go beyond His limits will be led into the Fire
to live forever, and it will be a humiliating torment!*

I150 Mohammed would take month-long retreats to be alone to perform
the Quraysh religious practices. After the retreat, he would circumambulate (circle the Kabah) and pray.

I152 At the age of forty, Mohammed began to have visions and hear
voices. His visions were first shown to him as bright as daybreak during his sleep in the month of Ramadan. Mohammed said that the angel
Gabriel came to him with brocade embroidered with writing and commanded him to read. "What shall I read?" The angel pressed him and said,
"Read." Mohammed said again, "What shall I read?" The angel pressed
him again tightly and again commanded, "Read!" Again the reply, "What
shall I read?"

The angel said:

> 96:1 *Recite: In the name of your Lord, Who created man from clots of
> blood.*
> 96:3 *Recite: Your Lord is the most generous, Who taught the use of the pen,
> and taught man what he did not know.*

T1150[1] Mohammed awoke from his sleep. Now, Mohammed hated
ecstatic poets and the insane. His thoughts were that he was now either a
poet or insane, that which he hated. He thought to kill himself by jumping
off a cliff. And off he went to do just that. Half-way up the hill, he saw a
being. "Mohammed," it said, "thou art the Apostle of Allah and I am Gabriel." He gazed at the angel and no matter which way he turned his head
the vision was before his eyes. Mohammed stood and watched for a long
time.

---

1. The T means that this is a margin reference from *The History of al-
Tabari.*

9

I153 He went back home to his wife, Khadija, and told her he was either crazy or a poet. She replied that he was neither, that perhaps the vision was true; he was a good man, and Allah would not play tricks on him. She was elated and said she thought him to be a prophet and set off to tell her Christian cousin about the visions.

T1150 When she told her cousin what Mohammed had said, he replied that this was wonderful news. He was sure the angel was Gabriel of the Torah (Old Testament) and that Mohammed was a prophet. She returned and told Mohammed what he had said. Mohammed felt better and went to the Kabah to pray. Khadija's Christian cousin, Waraqa, found him there and had him repeat his story. Waraqa agreed that surely Mohammed was a prophet.

Mohammed's visions, dreams, and voices were called revelations. A great many of these revelations were expressed in poetry that was easily memorized and recited. The recitations (*Koran* means recitation) were recorded and slowly grew into the complete Koran over the next twenty-three years.

THE FIRST CONVERT

I156 Mohammed's wife, Khadija, was the first convert. From the first she encouraged him, believed him. She knew him to be of good character and did not think him to be deceived or crazy.

Soon he stopped hearing voices or seeing visions and became depressed and felt abandoned. Then his visions started again and said:

> 93:1 *By the brightness of the noonday sun and by the night at its darkest, your Lord has not forgotten you, and He does not hate you.*
> 93:4 *Certainly the future will be better than the past, and in the end your Lord will be generous to you, and you will be satisfied.*

Then Mohammed began to tell others who were close to him of his visions.

PRAYER

I157 Mohammed began to pray with his new understanding. At first he did two prostrations with each prayer. Later he understood that he should use four prostrations per prayer and use two prostrations when he was traveling.

I158 Then, when he was on a mountain, he saw a vision in which Gabriel showed him how to do ritual ablutions (ritual cleansing with water) as a purification ritual before prayer. He went home and showed Khadija how he now understood the prayer rituals to be done and she copied him.

I158 Further inner visions made Mohammed pray at different times of the day.

THE FIRST MALES TO ACCEPT ISLAM

I159 A famine had overtaken the Quraysh and Mohammed's uncle, Abu Talib, had a large family. He was a well respected tribal leader but had fallen on hard times. Mohammed went to another uncle, Al Abbas, and they both went to Abu Talib and offered to help raise two of his children. One, Ali, went into Mohammed's house to be raised by him and Khadija. When Ali turned ten he joined Mohammed in his new religion, *Islam*, which means submission.

T1162 Mohammed, his wife, and his nephew, Ali, started praying at the Kabah with their new rituals of ablutions and prayer with prostrations. A visitor asked about this new ritual and was told it was a new religion and that Mohammed had said he would receive the treasures of Rome and Persia.

I160 Mohammed and Ali used to go to the edge of town to practice their new ritual prayers. One day Abu Talib came upon them and asked what were they doing. Mohammed replied, "Uncle, this is the religion of Allah, his angels, and his prophets and the religion of Abraham. Allah has sent me as an apostle to all mankind. You, my uncle, deserve that I should teach you the truth and call you to Islam." His uncle said he could not give up the religion of his ancestors but that he would support Mohammed. He also advised Ali, his son, to keep up his relation with Mohammed.

I161 Next, a freed slave joined Mohammed. After him, Abu Bakr joined the new religion. Abu Bakr was a very influential man among the Quraysh. He was well liked and had an easy manner. He knew more of the lineage of the Quraysh than any other man. Such knowledge was of extreme value in a tribe that worshiped its ancestors. In addition, Abu Bakr was a prosperous merchant. He counseled many of the tribe about business and tribal matters. He was the first Meccan to preach the new religion in public and was influential in bringing many Quraysh to Islam. Until this time, Mohammed had been as private as possible about his new religion.

I161 A new element was added to the religion. It was not enough to say that Allah was god, but it was also necessary to renounce the tribal gods as well. Islam was not just an affirmation but a denial and opposition as well.

PUBLIC PREACHING

4:14 But those who disobey Allah and His Messenger
and go beyond His limits will be led into the Fire to
live forever, and it will be a humiliating torment!

I166 Since the word was out, Mohammed began to openly preach his new doctrine. He had kept private for three years before going public.

> 15: 92 *By your Lord, We will certainly call them to account for all their deeds, so openly proclaim what you are commanded, and turn away from the polytheists.*
> 15:95 *Surely, We will defend you against those who scoff, who set up other gods with Allah.*
>
> 26:213 *Do not call upon any god but Allah, or you will be doomed. Rather, warn your close relatives, and be kind to the believers who follow you. If they disobey you, say, "I will not be responsible for your actions*
>
> 15:8 *We do not send the angels without good reason. If We did, the unbelievers would still not understand. Surely, We have sent down the message, and surely, We will guard it.*

Those who listened to Mohammed's message and joined him were called *Muslims,* which meant "those who have submitted."

I166 Mohammed called together about forty of his kinsmen. He addressed them, "I know of no Arab who has come to his people with a nobler message than mine. I have brought you the best in this world and the next. Allah has ordered me to call you to him. So which of you will co-operate with me in this matter?" Ali, fat in the belly and thin in the legs, with watery eyes, said, "Prophet of Allah, I will be your helper in this matter." Mohammed laid his hand on Ali's back and said, "This is my brother, my successor, and my executor among you. Hearken to him and obey him." The Quraysh laughed, got up, and said to Abu Talib, Mohammed's uncle, "He has ordered you to listen to your son and obey him." The Quraysh left.

I166 The Muslims went to the edge of Mecca in order to be alone to pray. One day a bunch of the Quraysh came upon them and began to mock them, and a fight started. One of the Muslims by the name of Sad,

12

chief of a Medinan Arab clan, picked up the jaw bone of a camel and struck one of the Quraysh with it and bloodied him. This violence was the first blood to be shed in Islam.

1167 When Mohammed spoke about his new religion, it did not cause any problems among the Meccans. After all, there were hundreds of religions in Mecca; it was a polytheistic culture and very religiously tolerant. Then Mohammed began to condemn their religion and rituals and worship. This was a new phenomenon. New religions could be added, and had been, but not to the detriment of others. The Meccans took offense and resolved to treat him as an enemy. Luckily, he had the protection of his influential uncle, Abu Talib.

1168 Some of the Quraysh went to Abu Talib and said to him, "Your nephew has cursed our gods, insulted our religion, mocked our way of life, criticized our civilization, attacked our virtues, and said our forefathers were ignorant and in error. You must stop him, or you must let us stop him. We will rid you of him." Abu Talib gave them a soft reply and sent them away.

1168 Mohammed continued to preach his religion and condemn the other religions. His relationship with the Meccans continued to deteriorate and men withdrew from him in dislike. He became the talk of Mecca and upset his tribe for saying the Quraysh's ancestors were burning in Hell and that the Meccans were wrong. It was not just that he was right or had a different way or even a better way but that they were wrong.

1168 Mohammed continued to preach Islam and his relations with his tribal kin grew worse and men drew away from him and his condemnation of who they were.

1168 Abu Talib called Mohammed to him and told him to spare him the burden of the pain of the Quraysh resentment. Mohammed told him that if they gave him the sun and the moon he would not change until Allah had made him victorious. Even if he died he would not quit. Abu Talib could not stand to censor his nephew and let him go with his consent.

1169 The Quraysh saw that Abu Talib would not help. Mohammed continued to preach Islam and attack them and their lives. Mecca was a small town; everybody knew everybody else. Islam had split the town of Mecca and divided the ruling and priestly tribe. The Quraysh were attacked at the very ground of their social being.

1169 The Quraysh were desperate and went with a desperate plan to Mohammed's protector. "Here is our strongest and most handsome man. Adopt him for his intelligence and support. Give us Mohammed. He has opposed both your and our religion, divided us as a people, and mocked us for who we are. Let us trade our best for your Mohammed so we can kill him. Then it would be man for man. Fair and just." Abu Talib would not give Mohammed up.

I170 Things got much worse. Now there was open hostility in the town. Quarrels increased; arguments got very heated. Complete disharmony dominated the town. The tribe started to abuse newly converted Muslims, but Mohammed's uncle was a respected elder and was able to protect them from serious harm.

THE FAIR

Mecca was a town with two sources of money. The first was trading. Mohammed had made his money in the caravan trade. The other was fees from pilgrims to the shrine of the Kabah, and fairs combined a little of both. All the tribes came for a fair where people would see old acquaintances and buy, sell, and trade goods. Since Mecca was one of several sacred or pilgrim sites, rituals for the different tribal gods were performed around the Kabah and Mecca.

I171 It was time for the fair and the Quraysh were in turmoil. They were desperate that the divisions and rancor that had come with Mohammed's preaching not spread to the other clans outside Mecca. A group of concerned Quraysh talked and decided to meet with Al Walid, a man of respect and influence. He told them that all the visitors would come to them and ask about this man Mohammed and what he was preaching. It was a foregone conclusion that Mohammed would preach.

I171 But what could they agree on to tell the visitors so that there could be one voice. What would they call him? Was he possessed? Crazy? An ecstatic poet? A sorcerer? Who was he? What was he? Finally they agreed that Mohammed was a sorcerer since he separated a son from his father or brother or wife or other family.

I171 They split up and went out on the roadsides of town to speak with the travelers before they even got to Mecca.

I171 Mohammed delivered a message from Allah about Al Walid, the leader of the unbelievers:

> 74:11 *Let me deal with my creations, whom I have given great riches and sons to sit by their side, and whose lives I have made smooth and comfortable. And still he wants me to give him more. No, I say. He is an enemy of Our revelations. I will impose a dreadful punishment on him because he plotted and planned.*
> 74:19 *Damn him! How he planned. Again, Damn him! How he planned.*

74:21 *Then he looked around and frowned and scowled and turned his back with vain pride and said, "This is nothing but old magic; it is the work of a mere mortal."*
74:26 *We will certainly throw him into Hell.*

1172 The plan of hurting Mohammed by warning the visitors just made everyone more curious. When they heard Mohammed's soaring words from the Koran, many visitors were impressed. When they left they took all the stories from Mecca, the Quraysh, the new Muslims, and, of course, Mohammed. Soon all of that part of Arabia was talking.

1178 Circumstances would soon prove fortuitous for Mohammed that the Arabs of Medina were attracted to his message. Since half the people of Medina were Jews, the Arabs of Medina were accustomed to talk of only one god.

ARGUING

CHAPTER 5

*4:80 Those who obey the Messenger obey Allah. As for those who
turn away from you, We have not sent you to watch over them.*

1183 Mohammed continued to preach the glory of Allah and condemn
the Quraysh religion. He told them their way of life was stupid and insulted their ancestors, cursed their gods, despised their religion, and divided
the community, setting one tribesman against another. The Quraysh felt
that this was all beyond bearing. Tolerance had always been their way:
many clans, many gods, many religions. Another religion was fine; why
did Mohammed demean the others?

1183 One day at the Kabah they were discussing Mohammed and his en-
mity toward them when Mohammed arrived. He kissed the Black Stone of
the Kabah and started past them as he circumambulated the Kabah. Each
time he passed by them they insulted him. On the third round, he stopped
and said, "Listen to me, by Allah I will bring you slaughter." The Quraysh
were stunned at his threat. They said, "Mohammed, you have never been
a violent man. Go away."

1184 The next day many of the Quraysh were at the Kabah when Mohammed arrived. They crowded around him and said, "Are you the one
who condemned our gods and our religion?" Mohammed answered that
he was the one. One of them grabbed him and Abu Bakr, Mohammed's
chief follower, pressed forward and said, "Would you kill a man for saying
that Allah is his Lord?" They let him go. This was the worst that Mohammed had been treated.

THE STRONG MAN ACCEPTS ISLAM

1185 Hamza was the strongest and most stubborn man of the Quraysh
and a great hunter. One day he returned from the hunt with his bow. It
was his custom to go to the Kabah and to circumambulate the shrine before he went home. After he performed his rituals, he stopped and talked
with the gathered Quraysh.

1186 Then, on the way home, he stopped to talk with a freedwoman of
the Quraysh. She told him of the abuse that Mohammed had received from
the Quraysh, in particular Abu Umara. Now, Hamza had been thinking

about becoming a Muslim and this was the tipping point. He rushed out in a rage to find Abu Umara who was back at the Kabah. Hamza charged him and struck him with his bow and bloodied his head. He challenged Abu Umara to try to get back at him and threatened him with greater harm if he ever insulted Mohammed again. Now that Mohammed had the muscle of the tribe's strongest man, he suffered less harassment.

A TRIBAL CHIEF TRIES TO CUT A DEAL

I186 One day while the Quraysh were in council, one of the chiefs, Utba, offered to approach Mohammed to see if he could make a deal that would please everybody. Things were only getting worse, so the others agreed for him to try. He went to the Kabah and found Mohammed. "Mohammed, you have come to us with an important matter, but you have divided the community, ridiculed our customs, and insulted our forefathers. See if any of my suggestions can help in this matter. If you want money, we will give you money. If you want honor, we will make you our king. If you are possessed, we will get you a physician."

I186 Mohammed said that he represented the only Allah, whose teachings were beautiful, and then he began to recite the glorious poetry and imagery of the Koran. The tribal chief was impressed with the beauty of Mohammed's words and left.

I186 When he returned to the Quraysh, he said, "Leave him alone; his words are beautiful. If other Arabs kill him, your problem is solved. If he becomes sovereign over all, you will share in his glory. His power will become your power and you can make money off his success." They replied that Mohammed had bewitched him.

MORE ARGUMENTS WITH THE MECCANS

I188, 189 Another group of Meccans sent for Mohammed to see if they could negotiate away this painful division of the tribes. They went over old ground and again Mohammed refused the money and power that were offered. He said they were the ones who needed to decide whether they wanted to suffer in the next world and he had the only solution. If they rejected him and his message, Allah would tend to them. One of the Quraysh said, "Well, if you speak for and represent the only true god, then perhaps this Allah could do something for us."

"This land is dry. Let your Allah send us a river next to Mecca," said another.

"We are cramped being next to the mountains. Let your Allah open up some space by moving the mountains back," said another.

"Our best members are dead. Let your Allah renew them to life and, in particular, send back the best leader of our tribe, Qusayy. We will ask Qusayy whether or not you speak truly," said another.

I189 Mohammed said he was sent as a messenger, not to do such work. They could either accept his message or reject it and be subject to the loss. Then one of them said, "If you won't use your Allah to help us, then let your Allah help you. Send an angel to confirm you and prove to us that we are wrong. As long as the angel is present, let him make Mohammed a garden and fine home and present him all the gold and silver he could need. If you do this, we will know that you represent Allah and we are wrong." The Quraysh wanted miracles as proof.

I189 Mohammed replied that he would not do so because such things were not what Allah had appointed him to do.

I189 Then one of the Quraysh said, "Then let the heavens be dropped on us in pieces as you say your Lord could do. If you do not, we will not believe." Mohammed said Allah could do that if Allah wished or he might not if he wished not.

I189 They then said, "Did not your Lord know that we would ask you these questions? Then your Lord could have prepared you with better answers. And your Lord could have told you what to tell us if we didn't believe. We hear that you are getting this Koran from a man named Al Rahman from another town. We don't believe in Al Rahman. Our conscience is clear. We must either destroy you or you must destroy us. Bring your angels and we will believe them."

I190 Mohammed turned and left. A cousin chased him and fell in beside him to talk. He said, "Mohammed, your tribe has made you propositions and you have rejected them. First, they asked you for things for themselves that they might see if you are true. They would have followed you. You did nothing. Then they asked you for things for yourself so they could see your superiority over them and prove your standing with Allah. You did nothing. Then they said to bring on the punishments that your Allah has threatened and with which you have frightened them. You did nothing. Personally, I will never believe until you get a ladder up to the sky and then climb it while I watch and four angels come and testify that you are truthful. But you know, even if you did all that, I still don't know if I would believe you."

1190 Mohammed went home, sad and depressed. He had hoped they sent for him to announce their submission to Allah and his teachings. Instead, they had offered more resistance and questions.

1191 Mohammed would go to the Kabah and tell the Meccans what terrible punishments Allah had delivered to others in history who had not believed his prophets.

> 73:15 *Certainly We have sent an apostle to bear witness against you [the world], just as We sent an apostle to Pharaoh, but Pharaoh rejected the apostle, and We punished him severely.*

That was now one of his constant themes: "Allah destroyed others like you who did not listen to men like me."

One of the Quraysh, Al Nadr, had been to Persia and learned many tales and sagas from the storytellers there. Al Nadr would announce, "I can tell a better tale than Mohammed." Then he would proceed to tell them ancient fables and stories of Persia. "In what way is Mohammed a better story-teller than I am?"

1192 The Quraysh decided to send their storyteller to the Jews in Medina to ask for help. It took eleven days to get to Medina and eleven days to return. This was not a casual quest, as it took the better part of a month for the trip and visit. At Medina, Al Nadr told the rabbis about Mohammed: what he did, what he said, and that he claimed to be a prophet. Since they had their own prophets they must know more about the subject than the Meccans. What questions could they ask Mohammed that would prove whether or not he was a prophet?

1192 The rabbis said, "Ask him these three questions. If he knows the answers then he is a prophet; if not, then he is a fake.

"Ask him, 'What is the spirit?'

"Ask him, 'What happened to the young men who disappeared in ancient days?'

"Ask him about the mighty traveler who reached the ends of the East and the West."

1192 Back in Mecca, they went to Mohammed and asked him the three questions. He promised to respond on the following day.

For fifteen days Mohammed waited for Gabriel to provide answers. The Meccans began to talk. Mohammed did not know what to do. He had no answers. Finally, he had a vision of Gabriel.

These were the Koranic answers to all the questions and statements of the Quraysh:

The question—what is the spirit?

17:85 *They will ask you about the spirit [probably the angel Gabriel]. Say: The spirit is commanded by my Lord, and you are given only a little knowledge about it. If We wished, We could take Our revelations away from you. Then you would find no one to intercede with us on your behalf except as a mercy from your Lord. Surely His kindness to you is great.*

With regard to the question about what happened to the young men in ancient times:

18:9 *Do you believe that the Sleepers of the Cave and the Inscription [an unknown reference] were among Our signs? When the youths [the Sleepers] took refuge in the cave, they said, "Lord, give us Your mercy and cause us to act rightly." We drew a veil over them depriving them of their senses for many years. Then We roused them so that We could know which would best determine the number of years they lived in the cave.*

18:13 *We tell you their story truthfully. They were youths who believed in their Lord, and We increased their ability to guide others. We gave strength to their hearts. Recall when they stood up and said, "Our Lord is the Lord of the heaven and the earth. We will worship no other god besides Him. If We did, then we would have certainly said an outrageous thing. Our people have taken other gods to worship besides Allah. Why don't they prove their existence? Who is more wicked than a person who makes up lies about Allah? When will you turn away from them and the things they worship besides Allah? Seek refuge in the cave. Your Lord will extend His mercy to you and cause your affairs to turn out for the best."*

18:17 *You may have seen the sun, when it rose, pass to the right of their cave and set to their left while they were in its spacious middle. This is one of the signs of Allah. Whomever Allah guides is rightly guided. Whomever He allows to stray will not find a friend to guide him.*

18:18 *While they were sleeping, you would have thought that they were awake [they slept with their eyes open]. We turned them on their right side and their left side. Their dog lay in the entrance with its paws stretched out. If you had come upon them, you would have certainly run away filled with terror of them. This was their condition before We awakened them so that they might question one another. One of them asked, "How long have you lingered here?" Some said, "We have been here a day or so." Others said, "Your Lord knows exactly how long you have lingered. One of you should take your money into the city and buy the best food possible. He should be courteous and should not let anyone know about you. If they should come upon you, they would either kill you or force you to return to their religion, in which case you would never prosper."*

18:21 *We made their existence known to the city so that they would know that Allah's promise is true and that there is no doubt about the Hour of Judgment. The people of the city argued amongst themselves about the affair. Some said, "We should construct a building over them. Their Lord knows all about them." The winners of the debate were those who said, "We will certainly build a temple over them."*

18:22 *Some say, "There were three, the dog being the forth." Others say, "Five, the dog was the sixth." Still others say, "There were seven, and a dog made eight." Say: My Lord knows the exact number. Only a few know the truth. So do not become involved in arguments about them except on matters that are clear, and do not consult any of them about the Sleepers.*

As to the question about the mighty traveler:

18:83 *They will ask you about Zul-Qarnain [Alexander, the Great]. Say: I will recite to you an account of him. We established his power in the land and gave him the means to achieve any of his aims. So he followed a path, until, when he reached the setting of the sun, he found it setting in a muddy pond. Near by he found a people. We said, "Zul-Qarnain, you have the authority to either punish them or to show them kindness."*

18:87 *He said, "Whoever does wrong, we will certainly punish. Then he will be returned to his Lord, Who will punish him with a terrible punishment. But whoever believes and does good deeds shall be given a wonderful reward, and We will give them easy commands to obey."*

18:89 *Then he followed another path, until, when he came to the rising of the sun, he found that it rose upon a people to whom We had given no protection from it. He left them as they were. We knew everything about him. Then he followed another path until, when he reached a place between two mountains, he found a people living in a valley who could scarcely understand a single word. They said, "Zul-Qarnain, the people of Gog and Magog are terrorizing the land. May we pay you tribute so that you will build a strong barrier between us and them?"*

18:95 *He said, "The power which my Lord has given me is better than your tribute. Help me, therefore, with manpower. I will build a strong barrier between you and them. Bring me blocks of iron." Later, when he had filled the gap between the two mountains, he said, "Blow with your bellows!" When it had become as red as fire, he said, "Bring me molten lead to pour over it." So the people of Gog and Magog were unable to climb over the barrier or to go through it. He said, "This is a mercy from my Lord, but when my Lord's promise comes to pass, He will destroy it, because my Lord's promises always come true."*

18:99 *On that day We shall let them surge against one another like waves. The trumpet will be blown, and We will gather them all together. On that day We shall present Hell for all the unbelievers to see—unbelievers whose eyes were veiled from My signs and who could not even hear. What?*

Do the unbelievers think that they can take My servants to be guardians besides me? We have prepared Hell to entertain the unbelievers.

The Quraysh had raised other questions. Mohammed was seeing and talking with angels. Could the Quraysh meet one of these messengers? If the god of Mohammed was so powerful, could not Mohammed do miracles such as furnishing more water for Mecca or making the sky fall? Since Allah could do all things, why could not Allah furnish Mohammed great wealth?

The Koran's response:

17:90 *They [the Meccans] say, "We will not believe in you until you cause a spring to gush forth from the earth for us; or until you have a garden of date trees and grape vines, and cause rivers to gush abundantly in their midst; or when you cause the sky to fall down in pieces, as you claim will happen; or when you bring us face to face with Allah and the angels; or when you have a house of gold; or when you ascend into heaven; and even then we will not believe in your ascension until you bring down a book for us which we may read." Say: Glory be to my Lord! Am I nothing except a man, a messenger?*

17:94 *What keeps men from believing when guidance has come to them but that they say, "Has Allah sent a man like us to be His messenger?" Say: If angels walked the earth, We would have sent down from heaven an angel as Our messenger. Say: Allah is a sufficient witness between you and me. He is well acquainted with His servants and He sees everything.*

Mohammed performed no miracles because Allah had not sent him for that. The proof of Mohammed's claims was the Koran.

The Quraysh had told Mohammed that the old stories from Persia were as good as his stories. So how were his stories proof of his being a messenger of God? The Koran's answer:

25:5 *They say, "These are ancient fables that he has written down. They are dictated to him morning and night."*
25:6 *Say: The Koran was revealed by Him who knows the secrets of the heavens and the earth. He is truly forgiving and merciful.*

The Quraysh were following the religion of their ancestors. Why was Mohammed's religion any better than theirs?

31:21 *Yet there are those who dispute Allah without knowledge nor a Scripture to enlighten them. And when it is said to them, "Follow what Allah has sent down," they say, "No, we will follow the path that we found our fathers following." Even if it is Satan inviting them into the doom of Fire?*

THE QURAYSH LISTEN TO MOHAMMED'S READING

1203 Three of the Meccans decided, each on his own, to sit outside Mohammed's house and listen to him recite the Koran and pray. As they left, they ran into each other. The Quraysh were opposing Mohammed and here they were sneaking around to hear him. So they agreed that, since they didn't want Mecca to know they were Quraysh listening to Mohammed, they would not do it again nor would they tell anyone what had happened. But on the next night they all three did the same thing, and on the third night they did it again. They then talked among themselves. The first one said, "I heard things I know and I know what was meant by them. And I heard things I don't know and I don't know what was intended by them." The second agreed. The third said he had always had a competition with one of Mohammed's recent converts. They had both fed the poor and helped the oppressed. They had always been equals, but now his friendly rival claimed he had a prophet and his friend did not. Hence, he was now superior. He said, "But I can never believe in this man, Mohammed."

1204 So the next time Mohammed called upon them to submit to Islam, they said, "Our hearts are veiled; we don't understand what you say. There is stuff in our ears so we can't hear you. A curtain divides us. You go follow your path and we will follow ours."

The Koranic response to their veiled hearts:

> 17:45 *When you recite the Koran, We place an invisible barrier between you and the unbelievers. We place veils over their hearts and deafness in their ears so that they do not understand it, and when you mention only your Lord, Allah, in the Koran, they turn their backs and flee from the truth. We know absolutely what they listen to when they listen to you, and when they speak privately, the wicked say, "You follow a mad man!" See what they compare you to. But they have gone astray and cannot find the way.*

TROUBLE

CHAPTER 6

*5:95 Obey Allah, and obey the Messenger, and be on your
guard. If you do turn back, know that our Messenger
is only bound to deliver a plain announcement.*

I217 All of the clans of the Quraysh began to persecute those Muslims
they had any power over. If Mohammed attacked them, they would attack him through his converts. One slave, Bilal (to become famous later),
was physically abused. He was placed in the hot sun with a huge rock on
his chest and told to deny Islam. He refused. This was repeated until Abu
Bakr, a chief Muslim, took notice and asked how long the owner would
abuse him. The owner said, "You are one of those who corrupted him.
You save him." So Abu Bakr offered to trade a stronger, black, non-Muslim
slave for Bilal. Then Abu Bakr freed Bilal. Abu Bakr did this with six other
Muslim slaves as well.

MIGRATION TO ETHIOPIA

I208 Since the Quraysh were resisting Islam and being hard on the Muslims, Mohammed sent many of his followers to Ethiopia as the Christian
king there was tolerant of their religion. Eighty or ninety Muslims left
Arabia to cross the Red Sea to Ethiopia.

I217 The Quraysh decided to send two men to Ethiopia to persuade the
king to send the Arabs back to Mecca.

I218 They took gifts of fine leather goods since leatherwork was prized
there. They gave the leatherwork to the generals of the king's army and
told them, "Foolish people from our country have moved here. They have
forsaken their religion and have not accepted yours. They have an invent-
ed religion. Our nobles have sent us to see the king so that he will return
these people to our country." The generals agreed and went to the king
to recommend he do as the Meccans had suggested. The king refused. To
surrender someone to whom he had extended protection would violate
his word, and his word was law and not to be changed.

UMAR ACCEPTS ISLAM

1224 Umar was a strong and stubborn man whom no one would attack. (Umar would later become a *caliph*—a supreme political and religious leader—and a successor when Mohammed died.) When some of the Muslims moved to Ethiopia, he was saddened to see them go. Up to that time he had joined in harassing the Muslims.

1225 His sister and her husband had both converted to Islam, but they concealed their conversion to avoid censure. One day Umar strapped on his sword and decided to go to the house where he knew Mohammed was holding a meeting with his converts. Umar had violence on his mind when he ran into a friend who asked him where he was going in such a rush. Umar told him, "I am going to cause trouble for Mohammed, the apostate, who mocked our religion and insulted our faith. I am going to kill him." His friend said, "You had better go straighten out the affairs of your own family. Your sister and brother-in-law have submitted to Islam."

1226 Umar wheeled and headed for his sister's house. She and her husband were listening to a Muslim reading from the Koran when Umar came storming up to the house. The reader jumped up and hid himself, and Umar's sister hid the page of the Koran under her thigh. But Umar had heard the reading. "What was that garbage I heard just now?" he said angrily. His sister said, "Oh, you didn't hear anything." Umar bellowed, "I hear that you and your husband have become followers of Mohammed." He grabbed his brother-in-law. His sister rose to defend her husband and Umar struck her hard. She cried out, "Yes, you are right. We have converted. Do as you will." Her face was bleeding and Umar regretted hitting her.

1226 He saw a corner of the hidden paper and said, "Give me that piece of paper, now." Umar could read, not a usual thing in Mecca. His sister said she was afraid to give it to him. Umar said not to worry; he would not destroy it. She replied, "You are unclean. Only the clean may touch the Koran." Umar washed his hands and started to read. He was captured by the lofty words and said, "What fine and noble speech this is."

1227 At that, the person who had been reading the Koran stepped out of hiding and said, "Come to Islam, Umar." Umar replied, "Lead me to Mohammed, that I may submit to Islam."

1227 Umar headed to the house where Mohammed was meeting with his companions. When Umar arrived and knocked at the door, one of the companions looked out and said in fear, "It is Umar and he has his sword on." Hamza, the strong man, said, "Let him in. We can handle him." Umar entered the room and said to Mohammed that he wished to become a Muslim.

1224 Now that he was a Muslim, Islam had two men, Umar and Hamza, who could defeat any man in combat. After that, there was less physical harassment of the Muslims.

THE BOYCOTT

1230 The Quraysh were frustrated. Mohammed attracted converts from the ancient religion of their forefathers and still attacked everything about the Meccans' way of life. He condemned their ancestors, gods, customs, religion, and community. What could they do about this division of their city and tribe? Someone came up with the idea of a boycott. They would allow no marriages between the Quraysh and the Muslims and no buying or selling of food. All of the points were agreed upon, and they went so far as to write up the boycott on paper and hang it in the Kabah. Mohammed cursed the writers, but the boycott went on for two or three years. Naturally, like all boycotts, it cut off the normal suppliers of food. Others merely stepped in and replaced the suppliers to the Muslims. In fact, Mohammed's mission went on undisturbed. He worked in both public and private during the entire time of the boycott.

1233 The battle of words went on. The Quraysh mocked, argued with, and laughed at Mohammed. Mohammed revealed new verses of the Koran that began to reflect the war of words. Abu Lahab and his wife are an example of how Mohammed and Allah responded. To understand the Koran's reference to them, it helps to know that Abu Lahab's wife threw some thorns in front of Mohammed, hence the reference to wood as fuel.

> 111:1 *Let the hands of Abu Lahab [Mohammed's uncle and an opponent] die and let him die! His wealth and attainments will not help him. He will be burned in Hell, and his wife will carry the firewood, with a palm fiber rope around her neck.*

Another Meccan won a place in the Koran:

> 104:1 *Woe to every slanderer and backbiter who gathers wealth and hordes it for the future. He certainly thinks he will keep his wealth forever. No! He certainly will be flung into Hell, and who will teach you what Hell is?*
> 104:6 *It is the Fire kindled by Allah that will rise above the hearts of the damned and close over them in towering columns.*

The tension Mohammed introduced into Mecca and his tribe became part of daily life.

1235 A Muslim blacksmith was owed money for his iron work and went to claim his debt. The debtor pointed out that in Mohammed's heaven there would be much luxury and gold, so he would meet the smith there and pay him with some of the excess gold lying around in heaven. The Koranic response:

> 19:77 *Have you seen someone who rejects Our signs and says, "I will certainly be given wealth and children?" Does he have knowledge of the unseen, or has he made peace with Allah? No! We will certainly record what he says and prolong his period of punishment. We will inherit the things he speaks of, and he will come before Us, poor and alone.*

1235 A Meccan told Mohammed, "You stop cursing our gods or we will start cursing your Allah." So Mohammed stopped cursing the Meccan gods. An ongoing theme of Mohammed was to tell of ancient civilizations that did not listen to their prophets and suffered terrible downfalls. A competing storyteller boasted that he could tell better stories. The Koran's reply:

> 45:6 *These are among the signs of Allah, which We truthfully recite to you. What teachings will they believe in if they reject Allah and his signs?*
> 45:7 *Woe to every sinful liar who hears the signs of Allah and still persists in vanity and pride as if he had never heard them. Tell him of a terrible punishment. When he becomes aware of Our signs he takes them for a joke. There will be a shameful penalty for people such as this. Hell is waiting for them. Neither their possessions nor the false gods can protect them in the least. They shall have a grievous punishment. Those who reject the signs and guidance of their Lord will receive a punishment of painful torment.*

1238 A Meccan took an old bone to Mohammed, crumbled it up, and blew the dust toward Mohammed. He asked, "Will your Allah revive this bone?" Mohammed said, "Yes, I do say that. Allah will resurrect this bone and you will die. Then Allah will send you to Hell!"

1239 Some Meccans approached Mohammed and said, "Let us worship what you worship. Then you worship what we worship. If what you worship is better than what we worship, then we will take a share of your worship. And if what we worship is better, then you can take a share of that." The Koran's reply:

> 109:1 *Say: O you unbelievers!*
> 109:2 *I do not worship what you worship, and you do not worship what I worship. I will never worship what you worship, and you will never worship what I worship. You to your religion, me to my religion.*

THE SATANIC VERSES

T1192 Mohammed was always thinking of how he could convert all the Meccans. It came to him that the three gods of the Quraysh could intercede with Allah on their behalf. As Mohammed put it, "These are the exalted high flying cranes whose intercession is approved." The Meccans were delighted. The Muslims were happy. When Mohammed led prayers at the Kabah, all the Meccans, Muslim and non-Muslim, took part. The Quraysh hung about after the combined service and remarked how happy they were. The tribe had been unified in worship, as before Islam.

T1192 When the news reached Ethiopia, some of the Muslims started for home. But then trouble appeared. Mohammed's inner voice told him he had been wrong. Meccan gods could have no part in his religion. Satan had made him say those terrible words about how the other gods could help Allah.

> 22:52 *Never have We sent a prophet or messenger before you whom Satan did not tempt with evil desires, but Allah will bring Satan's temptations to nothing. Allah will affirm His revelations, for He is knowing and wise. He makes Satan's suggestions a temptation for those whose hearts are diseased or for those whose hearts are hardened. Truly, this is why the unbelievers are in great opposition so that those who have been given knowledge will know that the Koran is the truth from their Lord and so that they may believe in it and humbly submit to Him. Allah will truly guide the believers to the right path.*

> 53:23 *These are mere names. You and your fathers gave them these names. Allah has not acknowledged them. They follow only their own conceits and desires, even though their Lord has already given them guidance.*

T1192 The retraction by Mohammed made relations between the Muslims and Meccans far worse than it had ever been. The Koran mentions a tree of Zaqqum which guards heaven. It represented a terrible barrier. After the retraction some Meccans started mocking it and said the tree of Zaqqum was a date palm that gave buttered dates. The Koran replied to this little joke:

> 44:43 *Surely the Zaqqum tree [the tree of Hell] will be food for the sinners. Like molten brass, it will boil in their bellies like the boiling of scalding water. (It will be said) "Seize him and drag him down to the middle of Hell. Torment him by pouring boiling water on his head." (Say) Taste this: You thought that you were powerful and honorable! This is the thing that you doubted.*

PROTECTION

1244 Like Mohammed, Uthman (later to become a caliph) had protection from a powerful tribal leader. In Arabic society there were rules
governing how tribes, clans, and individuals extended protection, and
most of Uthman's new Muslim brothers did not have the protection Uthman enjoyed. In sympathy with his fellow Muslims, Uthman decided to
forfeit his protection. He went to his uncle and told him thenceforth Allah would be his sole defense. His uncle said they must go to the mosque
(Kabah) and announce his decision to the community. The oath of protection had been public, and the renunciation would have to be public as
well. Uthman told those there that his uncle was an honorable man but
Uthman wanted only the protection of Allah.

1244 Then one of the Meccans repeated a verse, "Everything but Allah
is vain."

"True," said Uthman.

The Meccan quoted further, "And everything lovely must inevitably
cease."

1214 This was apparently a contradiction of Uthman's new faith. "You
are a liar!" he cried. "The joy of Paradise will never cease." A Meccan who
was there said, "Oh, men of the Quraysh, you never used to argue like
this. What is going on?" Another Quraysh said, "It is one of those fools
who follow Mohammed. They have left our religion and insult us at every
turn. Just ignore him." Then Uthman objected vigorously. A man of the
Quraysh stood up and hit Uthman in the eye with a mighty blow and
blackened it. Uthman's uncle said, "See, if you had remained in my protection, this would not have happened." Uthman replied, "No, my good eye
needs what happened to my bad eye for Allah's sake. My Allah is stronger
than you." His uncle said, "Come on, my nephew. My protection is always
available if you ask." Uthman strode out of the Kabah.

1246 Abu Bakr decided that he would emigrate rather than put up with
the daily harassment that went on between the Quraysh and the Muslims.
He decided to go to Ethiopia. Traveling on the road he fell in with an Arab,
Al Dughunna, whose brother was the head of a powerful clan. When Al
Dughunna found out that Abu Bakr was leaving Mecca, he told him to
come back to Mecca with him and he would offer Bakr protection so that
he would not be bothered by the other Meccans.

1246 And so Bakr went back to Mecca and Al Dughunna publicly made
known his protection of Abu Bakr. Abu Bakr had the habit of reading the Koran in public places and crying as he read. This affected the
women and the young of the Quraysh. So one of the Quraysh went to Al

Dughunna and asked why he had given protection to one who was injuring the Quraysh with his public displays of weeping over the Koran. "Tell him to go to his own house and do as he pleases but stay out of public."

I246 Al Dughunna did so. He told Bakr he did not mean to harm the Quraysh by protecting him. Why didn't he just go home and be pious there? He should stop the public displays of piety. Abu Bakr asked him to retract his protection instead. And that is what Al Dughunna did.

I246 After that, one of the Quraysh threw dust at Abu Bakr while he was at the Kabah. Such was the persecution of the Muslims by the Quraysh.

ENDING THE BOYCOTT

I248, 249 The boycott was a hard piece of business for the Quraysh. Mecca was a small town, and many of those being boycotted were friends and family by marriage or kin. Just as with all boycotts there had been subtle cheating and help for those being boycotted. It was hard to eat well, buy new clothes, and marry, all the while knowing that others in the small town were suffering from the boycott. There began to be quiet talk about ending the boycott. Because many did not want friends and family to suffer, they began to hold clandestine meetings on the subject. A large meeting was held at the Kabah, where the boycott document was still posted. A boycott needs a very large majority to succeed and there wasn't one in Mecca. The Quraysh were too soft-hearted to press the issue and the boycott failed.

The Quraysh had always had a moon god called Allah. They had always started all documents with the phrase, "In thy name, O Allah." So both Muslims and non-Muslims argued with each other and cursed each other and swore in the name of Allah.

THE POET'S PROFITABLE SUBMISSION

I252 Al Dausi was a poet of some standing in Arabia, and when he visited Mecca he was warned to stay away from Mohammed. Mohammed had done the Quraysh much harm and broken the harmony of the tribe. Al Dausi was warned that Mohammed might bring such divisions to his family as well. When he went to the mosque, however, Mohammed was there. Since he had been warned about him, he was curious to hear what Mohammed said when he prayed. He liked what he heard and followed Mohammed home. They spoke for some time and Al Dausi decided to submit to Islam.

I253 He returned home. His father was old and came to greet his son. Al Dausi said to him, "Go away, Father, for I have nothing to do with you or you with me." His father said, "Why, my son?" Al Dausi said, "I have become a Muslim." The father replied, "Well, then, I shall do so as well."

1253 His father then entered his home and told his wife, "Leave me. I will have nothing to do with you." She cried, "Why?" Al Dausi said, "Islam has divided us and I now follow Mohammed." She replied, "Then your religion is my religion." He then instructed her in Islam.

1254 Al Dausi preached to his tribe but without the success he'd had with his family. He went back to Mecca and spoke with Mohammed. "Mohammed, my people are too frivolous for Islam. Put a curse on them." Mohammed told him to go back and continue to preach Islam. Some success followed. Years later when Mohammed left Mecca and became a military success, Al Dausi and his group of eighty families of converts showed up in Medina in time for the capture of Khaybar. The Jews of Khaybar were rich, and much treasure was taken from them, and Al Dausi and his group got to share in the wealth taken by war.

SOME CHRISTIANS FROM ETHIOPIA SUBMIT TO ISLAM

1259 Some Christians from Ethiopia came to see Mohammed in Mecca. After extended conversations, they decided to accept Islam. Abu Jahl of the Quraysh said to them, "What a wretched group you are. Your people sent you here to get information, and what do you do? You go and renounce your religion and believe everything Mohammed tells you. What a stupid bunch you are." They gave him a pleasant reply and went back to Ethiopia.

MOHAMMED'S SOURCE?

1260 There was one Christian in Mecca Mohammed took particular interest in, a slave who ran a booth in the market. Mohammed would often speak with him at length. This led the Quraysh to say that what Mohammed said in the Koran actually came from the Christian slave. The Koran's response:

> 16:103 *We know that they say, "It is a man that teaches him." The man [his name is uncertain] they point to speaks a foreign language while this is clear Arabic.*
> 16:104 *Allah will not guide those who do not believe, and they will have a painful punishment. Those who do not believe in Allah's revelations forge lies. They are the liars.*

The Meccans asked Mohammed why his angel never appeared to them along with Mohammed. They would like to see, hear, and speak with this Gabriel. Other Meccans made fun of Mohammed and mocked him. The Koran:

> 6:8 *They say, "Why has an angel not been sent down to him?" If We had sent down an angel, their judgment would have condemned the unbelievers suddenly, and no time would have been granted to them to repent. If We had made him an angel, We would have sent him as a man, and We would have caused confusion in a matter in which they are already confused. Messengers before you were mocked, but the scoffers were destroyed by the thing they mocked.*

THE NIGHT JOURNEY

1264 Mohammed said that one night, as he lay sleeping, an angel nudged him with his foot. Mohammed awoke, saw nothing, and went back to sleep. This happened again. Then it happened a third time. Mohammed awoke and Gabriel took his arm. They went out the door and before them was a white animal, half mule and half donkey with wings on its feet so it could move to the horizon at one step. Gabriel put Mohammed on the white animal and off they went to Jerusalem to the site of the Temple.

1264 There at the Temple were Jesus, Abraham, Moses, and prophets from Christian and Jewish scripture. Mohammed led them in prayer. Gabriel brought Mohammed two bowls. One was filled with wine and the other with milk. Mohammed took the one with milk and drank it. That was the right choice.

1265 When Mohammed told this story at the Kabah, the Quraysh hooted at the absurdity of it. Actually, some of the Muslims found it too hard to believe and left Islam. One of them went to Abu Bakr and told him Mohammed had visited Jerusalem the night before. Bakr said they were lying. They told him to go and hear for himself. Mohammed was at the mosque now telling his story, and Abu Bakr said, "If he says it then it is true. He tells me of communication with Allah that comes to him at all hours of the day and night. I believe him."

1265 Mohammed's wife said Mohammed never left the bed that night; however, his spirit soared. The Koran had something to say to those Muslims who did not believe Mohammed.

1266 Mohammed reported that Abraham looked exactly like him. Moses was a ruddy-faced man, tall and thin, with curly hair. Jesus was light-skinned with a reddish complexion and freckles and lank hair.

1268 Mohammed next reported that, after the prayers in Jerusalem, Gabriel brought a fine ladder. He and Gabriel climbed the ladder until they came to one of the gates of heaven called Gate of the Watchers. An angel was in charge there and had under his command twelve thousand angels. Each of those twelve thousand angels had twelve thousand angels under him. The guardian angel asked Gabriel who Mohammed was. When Gabriel said it was Mohammed, the angel wished Mohammed well.

1268 All the angels who greeted Mohammed smiled and wished him well, except for one. Mohammed asked Gabriel who was the unsmiling angel. He was Malik, the Keeper of Hell. Mohammed asked Gabriel to ask Malik if he would show him Hell. So Malik removed the lid to Hell and flames blazed into the air. Mohammed quickly asked for the lid to be put back.

1269 At the lowest heaven sat a man watching the spirits of men passing by. To one he would say, "A good spirit from a good body." And to another spirit he would say, "An evil spirit from an evil body." Mohammed asked who the man was. It was Adam reviewing the spirits of his children. The spirit of a believer excited him and the spirit of an infidel disgusted him.

1269 Mohammed saw men with lips like a camel. In their hands were flaming hot coals. They would shove the coals into their mouths and the burning coals came out of their rectums: these were those who had stolen the wealth of orphans. Then he saw the family of the pharaoh with huge bellies, and he saw women hanging by their breasts: these women had birthed bastards while married. Mohammed said that Allah hates women who birth bastards because they are outsiders who deprive the true sons of their inheritance and they learn the secrets of the harem, which is to be totally private from outsiders.

1270 Mohammed was then taken up to the second heaven where he saw Jesus and his cousin, John, son of Zechariah. In the third heaven he saw Joseph, son of Jacob. In the fourth heaven, Mohammed saw Idris (a prophet). In the fifth heaven was Aaron, son of Imran, handsome with a long beard and white hair. In the sixth heaven was a dark man with a hooked nose. This was Moses. [*Ed.* There is no accounting for the seemingly contradictory terms "ruddy" and "dark" describing Moses in 1266 and 1270.] In the seventh heaven was a man sitting on a throne in front of a mansion.

1270 Every day seventy thousand angels went into the mansion, not to come out until the day of resurrection. The man on the throne looked just like Mohammed; it was Abraham. Abraham took Mohammed into Paradise where there was a beautiful woman with red lips. Mohammed asked whom she belonged to, for she was very attractive to him. She was

Zaynab, the wife of his adopted son, Zayd. When he got back, Mohammed told him of this.

I271 When Gabriel took Mohammed to each of the heavens and asked heaven's guardian angel for permission to enter, he had to say whom he had brought and whether they had a mission. The guardian angel would then say, "Allah grant him life, brother, and friend." When Mohammed got to the seventh heaven Allah gave him the duty of fifty prayers a day. When he returned and passed Moses, Moses asked him how many prayers Allah had given him. When Moses heard that it was fifty, he said, "Prayer is a weighty matter and your people are weak. Go back and ask your Lord to reduce the number for you and your community." Mohammed went back and got the number reduced to forty. When he passed Moses, the same conversation passed. This repeated until Allah reduced the number to five. Moses tried to get Mohammed to go back and get the number reduced even further, but Mohammed felt ashamed to ask for less.

THE MOCKERS

I272 Mohammed continued to preach Islam and condemn the old Arabic religions. There were those of the Quraysh who defended their culture and religion and argued with Mohammed. Mohammed called them mockers and cursed one of them, "O Allah, blind him and kill his son."

The response in the Koran to those who argued with Mohammed:

> 15:94 *By your Lord, We will certainly call them to account for all their deeds, so openly proclaim what you are commanded, and turn away from the polytheists.*
> 15:95 *Surely, We will defend you against those who scoff, who set up other gods with Allah. But they will come to know. We know that your heart is troubled at their words, but celebrate the praises of your Lord, and be one of those who bow down in adoration. And serve your Lord until death overtakes you.*

I272 A common tale in Islam is that one day Mohammed stood with the angel, Gabriel, as the Quraysh performed the rituals of their religion. Among them were those who defended their culture and religion. When the first Quraysh passed by Gabriel, Gabriel threw a leaf in his face and blinded him; he caused the second one to get dropsy, which killed him; he caused the third man to develop an infection which killed him. Later, Gabriel caused the fourth man to step on a thorn that killed him, and he caused a brain disease to kill the last man who dared to not worship Allah.

MOHAMMED'S PROTECTOR AND MOHAMMED'S WIFE DIE

1278 Mohammed's protector was his uncle, Abu Talib. When he fell ill, some of the leaders of the Quraysh went to his bedside and said to him, "You are one of our leaders and are near dying. Why don't you call Mohammed to see if we can't work out some solution to the pain and division in our tribe? Why doesn't he leave us alone, not bother us, and we will not bother him? We will have our religion, and he can have his."

1278 So Abu Talib called Mohammed to his side, saying, "Nephew, these men have come so that you can give them something and they can give you something." Mohammed said, "If they will give me one word, they can rule the Persians and the Arabs, but they must accept Allah as their Lord and renounce their gods."

1278 The Quraysh said, "He will give us no agreement. Let Allah judge between us," and they left.

1278 Mohammed turned his attention to his dying uncle. He asked him to become a Muslim, and then Mohammed could intercede for him on judgment day. His uncle told him, "The Quraysh would say that I only accept Islam because I fear death, but I should say it just to give you pleasure." He drifted off, but as he died his lips moved. His brother put his head close to Abu Talib and listened. He then said, "Nephew, my brother said what you wished him to say." Mohammed's reply was, "I did not hear him." Mohammed left. The man who had raised Mohammed, protected him from danger, and taught him his occupation as businessman died. Later references state that Abu Talib went to Allah's Hell.

After Abu Talib's death, the pressure on Mohammed was greater. As an example, one of the Quraysh threw dust at Mohammed as an insult. The death of his wife had no political effect, but it was a blow to Mohammed. His wife, Khadija, was his chief confidante and she consoled him.

MARRIAGE

M113[1] About three months after the death of Khadija, Mohammed married Sauda, a widow and a Muslim.

M113 Abu Bakr had a daughter, Aisha, who was six years old. Soon after marrying Sauda, Mohammed was betrothed to Aisha, who was to become his favorite wife. Mohammed was in his early fifties. The consummation would take place when she turned nine.

---

1. The M refers to Sir William Muir's, *The Life of Muhammad*. The number is the page number.

M031,5977[1] *Aisha reported Mohammed's having said: I saw you [Aisha] in a dream for three nights when an angel brought you to me in a silk cloth and he said: Here is your wife, and when I removed the cloth from your face, lo, it was yourself, so I said: If this is from Allah, let Him carry it out.*

---

1.   An M reference with two parts is from Abu Muslim's Hadith, *Sahih Muslim.*

POLITICAL BEGINNINGS

CHAPTER 7

*8:20 Believers! Be obedient to Allah and His messenger, and
do not turn your backs now that you know the truth. Do
not be like the ones who say, "We hear," but do not obey.*

1279 After Abu Talib's death, Mohammed needed political allies. He went to the city of Taif, about fifty miles away, with one servant. In Taif he met with three brothers who were politically powerful. Mohammed called them to Islam and asked them to help him in his struggles with those who would defend their native religions.

1279 One brother said that if Mohammed were the representative of Allah he would go rip off the covering of the Kabah, Allah's shrine.

1279 The second brother said, "Couldn't Allah have found someone better than you to be a prophet?"

1279 The third brother said, "Don't let me even speak to you. If you are the prophet of Allah as you say you are, then you are too important for me to speak with. If you are not, then you are lying. And it is not right to speak with liars."

1280 Since they could not agree, Mohammed asked the three brothers to keep their meeting private. But Taif was a small town and within days everyone knew of Mohammed's presence. Taif was a very religious town following the old ways of the Arabs. Mohammed kept condemning them and their kind, until one day a mob gathered and drove him out of town, pelting him with stones.

1281 Half-way back to Mecca, he spent the night. The Koran says that jinns[1] came to hear him pray when he arose for his night prayer:

46:29 *We sent a company of jinn so that they might hear the Koran. When the reading was finished, they returned to their people with warnings. They said, "O, people! We have heard a scripture sent down since the days of Moses verifying previous scriptures, a guide to the truth and the straight path. O, people! Hear the Messenger of Allah and believe Him that He will forgive your faults and protect you from tormenting punishment."*

---

1. Islam has an entire world of spirits called jinns (genies). They can influence humans for good or bad.

37

PREACHING BACK IN MECCA

1282 When the fairs returned to Mecca, Mohammed went out to the crowd of visitors and told them he was the prophet of Allah and brought them the Koran, saying they should abandon their ancient religions and follow him. When he was finished with his preaching, a Quraysh who followed him told the audience to ignore Mohammed, that he was just trying to get them to abandon their ancestors' religions.

1283 One of the chiefs of a visiting tribe was taken with the power of Mohammed. He said, "By Allah, if I could take this man from the Quraysh, I could eat up all of Arabia with him." He asked Mohammed, "If I give allegiance to you and Allah gives you victory over your enemies, will we have authority over you?" Mohammed replied that Allah gave authority where he pleased. The chief said back, "So we protect you with our arms and lives and you reap the benefit! Thanks, but no thanks."

1285 Mohammed approached one visitor, who said, "Perhaps you have something like what I have." He handed Mohammed a scroll of Luqman[1]. Mohammed said, "This is fine, but I have something better, a Koran which Allah has revealed to me." The visitor said Mohammed's Koran was fine poetry, but he was not converted.

THE BEGINNING OF POWER AND JIHAD IN MEDINA

Medina was about a ten-day journey from Mecca, but since ancient days the Medinans had come to Mecca for the fairs. Medina was half Jewish and half Arab, and there was ongoing tension between the two. The Jews worked as farmers and craftsmen and were literate. They were the wealthy class, but their power was slowly waning. In times past the Arabs had raided and stolen from the Jews. The Jews retaliated by saying that one day a prophet would come and lead them to victory over the Arabs. In spite of the tension, the Arab tribe of Khazraj were allies with the Jews.

1286 When the members of the Khazraj met Mohammed, they said among themselves, "This is the prophet the Jews spoke of. Let us join ranks with him before the Jews do." They became Muslims. Their tribe was rancorous and divided, and they hoped that Islam could unite them. Soon every house in Medina had heard of Islam.

1289 The next year when the Medinan Muslims returned to Mecca, they took an oath to Mohammed, the first oath of Aqaba (so named because of the location outside Mecca where the pilgrims had set up camp; the "oath

---

1. Luqman was a philosopher and a writer of wisdom.

of Aqaba" is an established term in Islamic literature). They returned to Medina and soon many Medinans submitted to Islam. This first oath of Aqaba was called the oath of women and was not a blood oath.

1294 The next year at the fair in Mecca, many of the new Muslims from Medina showed up. During the early part of the night about seventy of them left the caravan to meet with Mohammed. He recited the Koran and said, "I invite your allegiance on the basis that you protect me as you would your children." (This was a blood oath.) The Medinans gave their oath. One of them then asked about their now severed ties to the Jews of Medina. If they helped Mohammed with arms and they were successful, would he go back to Mecca? Mohammed smiled and said, "No, blood is blood, and blood not to be paid for is blood not to be paid for." Blood revenge and its obligation were common to them. "I will war against those who war against you and be at peace with those at peace with you."

1297 Mohammed told them to appoint twelve leaders to take charge of the people's affairs.

1299 One of the Medinans said to those taking the pledge, "Do you realize what you are committing yourselves to in pledging your support to this man? It is war against all. Quit now if you think you will give him up after losing your property and your best are killed. But if you think you will be loyal to your oath even if you do lose your property and your best are killed, then take him, for it will profit you now and in Paradise." They asked what they would receive for their oath; Mohammed promised them Paradise. They all shook hands on the deal.

> B4,52,207 *I [Salama] gave the pledge of allegiance to Allah's Apostle and then I moved to the shade of a tree. When the number of people around the Prophet diminished, he said, "O Ibn Al-Akwa! Will you not give to me the pledge of allegiance?"*
>
> *I replied, "O Allah's Apostle! I have already given to you the pledge of allegiance."*
>
> *He said, "Do it again." So I gave the pledge of allegiance for the second time."*
>
> *I asked, "O Abu Muslim! For what did you give the pledge of allegiance on that day?"*
>
> *He replied, "We gave the pledge of allegiance for death."*

The Medinans retired to the caravan for the night.

1304 The second oath of Aqaba had conditions of war that were not in the first oath. Now the Muslims of Medina were bound to war against all for Allah and Mohammed. For faithful service they would go to Paradise for complete obedience.

I301 In the morning the leaders of the Quraysh came to the caravan. They had heard that the Medinans had come to invite Mohammed to Medina and had pledged themselves to war against the Quraysh. The Quraysh wanted no part of war with the Medinans. But there were Medinans in the caravan who had not heard of the pledge and were puzzled by their protests.

I301 One of the Quraysh was wearing a new pair of sandals. A Medinan Muslim called out to a friend, "You need to get some new sandals like the ones on this young Quraysh." The Quraysh took them off and threw them at the speaker. "Whoa, don't get them riled up," said the friend. "Give him back his sandals." "No," said the Muslim. "It is a good omen. I shall steal what he has in war."

BACK IN MEDINA

I304 Back in Medina the Muslims now practiced their new religion openly, but most of the Arabs still practiced their ancient tribal religions. The Muslims would desecrate the old shrines and ritual objects. They broke into houses and stole the ritual objects and threw them into the latrines. On one occasion they killed a dog and tied the dog's body to the ritual object and thew it into the latrine.

THE OPENING WORDS OF WAR

I313 Until now the tension in the Quraysh tribe over the new religion had been resolved by words. Curses and insults had been exchanged: Mohammed condemned the ancient religion and customs on an almost daily basis, and the Quraysh mocked Mohammed and abused lower class converts. What blood had been drawn had been in the equivalent of a brawl. Dust had been thrown in the face of Mohammed, but no real violence had occurred and no one had died. Then there came a new kind of word:

> 22:39 *Those who have been attacked are given permission to fight because they have been persecuted, and surely Allah is able to make them victorious.*

And the end of war would come when Islam ruled:

> 22:41 *But surely Allah will help those who help Him in His cause. Allah is strong and mighty. Allah will surely help those who, once we establish them as leaders in the land, pray regularly and pay the poor tax and command what is right and forbid what is wrong. And the final outcome of all things is in Allah's hands.*

This was jihad, fighting in Allah's Cause. Those who resisted Mohammed were worse than killers, and their reward would be death and Hell.

2:190 *Fight for the sake of Allah those that fight against you, but do not attack them first. Allah does not love aggressors.*

2:191 *Slay them wherever you find them. Drive them out of the places [Medina] from which they drove you. Idolatry is more grievous than bloodshed. But do not fight them within the precincts of the Holy Mosque unless they attack you there; if they attack you put them to the sword. Thus shall the unbelievers be rewarded: but if they mend their ways, know that Allah is forgiving and merciful.*

2:193 *Fight against them until idolatry is no more and Allah's religion reigns supreme. But if they desist, fight none except the evil-doers.*

EMIGRATION

I314 Allah had given permission to fight. The Muslim Medinans had pledged to support Mohammed in war and help the Muslims from Mecca. The Muslims in Mecca left and went to Medina.

MOHAMMED IN MEDINA

MEDINA

CHAPTER 8

*9:63 Do they not know that whoever opposes Allah
and His Messenger will abide in the Fire of Hell, where
they will remain forever? This is the great shame.*

1324 All of the Muslims, except for Mohammed, Ali, and Abu Bakr, had left for Medina. The Quraysh saw that Mohammed had new allies outside of Mecca and their sphere of influence. They feared that Mohammed would join the Muslims in Medina and they knew that his oath of allegiance included war with the Quraysh and Mecca. So the Quraysh assembled as a council to decide what to do.

1324 The council opened with the fact that Mohammed had new allies outside the tribe, so the Quraysh could be suddenly attacked. What was the best course of action? One suggestion was that they arrest him—put him behind bars and wait for nature to take its course. One day he would die of natural causes and they would be rid of him. But what if the news leaked out? There was no way to keep it secret. At some point his followers would attack the jail and free him, and Mohammed would then be a hero and his numbers would grow and threaten the Quraysh.

1325 "Well," they asked, "why not just drive him out of the country?" The Quraysh did not care to hurt him; they just wanted to be left alone so they could go back to the harmonious life they had enjoyed before Mohammed. Still, they recognized his ability to attract followers with fine speech and poetic language. Whatever desert-dwelling Bedouin tribe he settled with would become contaminated with his ideas and convert to Islam. Then Mohammed, with his new army of followers, could attack Mecca and take over the Quraysh's power and authority. Mohammed would rule.

1325 One elder had a better idea: let each clan put forth the strongest of their clan, provide each champion a sword, and let each of them strike a blow so that no one clan would have the problems of revenge and blood money that were the currency of tribal law. His clan could not fight them all, and all the clans together would share the blood-money fine. Mohammed would be dead and the consequences would be small change. This was the plan that the leaders of the Quraysh chose.

1326 In a town as small as Mecca, with a meeting as large as this council and an agenda the death of the man who had put everyone in turmoil for ten years, there was no way the decision would remain a secret. Mohammed knew within hours of the meeting what had happened.

PROTECTION BY ALLAH

There is a category of miracles regarding the divine protection of Mohammed, the ideal *imam* (religious leader). Following are some examples of these "protection miracles."

1326 Mohammed was warned by Gabriel not to sleep in his bed one particular night. That night Mohammed heard men gathering outside his house, so he had Ali lie upon his bed while Mohammed stayed awake.

1326 The leader of the Quraysh band told the assembled assassins that Mohammed taught that those who followed him would be kings of the Arabs and Persians and would die rich and be admitted to Paradise. Those who didn't follow him would be killed and burn forever in Hell. Mohammed came out of the dark and said, "That is what I say." Allah blinded the assembled men when Mohammed threw dust at them. He then was free to go.

1326 After he left, someone came upon the assembled band and asked what they were doing. "Waiting for Mohammed," they said. The person pointed out that Mohammed was gone and that all of them had dust on their heads. They reached up and felt the dust on their heads. The Koran's version:

> 8:30 *Remember the unbelievers who plotted against you and sought to have you taken prisoner or to have you killed or banished. They made plans, as did Allah, but Allah is the best plotter of all.*

LEAVING MECCA

1327 It was time to leave town. Abu Bakr was a man of some wealth and had wanted to leave Mecca before now, but Mohammed had told him to wait and perhaps he would have a companion. Abu Bakr loved Mohammed without reservation and hoped Mohammed himself would be the companion. To that end, he had prepared two camels for the journey.

1327 It was the custom for Mohammed to appear at Abu Bakr's house early in the morning or late at night. When he showed up at noon, Abu Bakr knew something was up. Abu Bakr's two daughters were in the room and Mohammed asked them to leave. Abu Bakr protested that his daughters would inform no one of anything that was said. Mohammed agreed they could stay and then said it was time to leave. Abu Bakr was delighted at the prospect of being Mohammed's companion on the road to Medina, and he wept with joy.

1329 Ali stayed behind to finish up some of Mohammed's business details. Mohammed and Abu Bakr left by the back window and headed for a cave in a small mountain near Mecca. Abu Bakr's son was left behind to gather intelligence about any plans for pursuit. His servant was to feed his flock of sheep and bring them to the cave that night. One of Abu Bakr's daughters brought food at night. They stayed in the cave for three days.

1329 When the Quraysh realized that Mohammed had fled, they offered a reward of a hundred camels to the person who could bring him back. During the day, Abu Bakr's son would listen to gossip around town and bring back the news at night. After three days the talk died down. Mohammed, Abu Bakr, a guide, and a servant headed out on the ten-day trip to Medina.

1335 Ali remained in Mecca until he had finished taking care of details of Mohammed's business as a trader with Syria. He then set out for Medina. On the road, he stayed in a town where Islam was just getting started. The house next door had an unmarried Muslim woman in it, and Ali noticed that for two nights a man came to her house and gave her something. He was suspicious about what was going on and asked her about it. She replied that the man who came to the door was a Muslim who would sneak into the homes of followers of traditional Arab religions and steal the objects on their shrines. She would burn them as fuel for cooking.

1336 About a week later, Ali joined Mohammed in Medina and set to work building the first mosque. It was time for Mohammed to choose a place to live. All the Medinan Muslims had asked him to stay with them. Mohammed mounted his camel, loosened the reigns, and let the camel wander. It finally stopped at the home of a Muslim, and Mohammed got off his camel. That was where he would stay.

1337 All the Muslims, including Mohammed, pitched in and prepared the mud brick mosque and home. During the construction, one of the men complained that the other workers were killing him by working him too hard. Mohammed ran his hand through the other man's curly hair and said, "Alas! It is not they who will kill you but a wicked band of men." Already, Mohammed's mind was on war. The man was later killed in a battle ordered by Mohammed.

There were now two groups of Muslims in Medina. One became known as the Immigrants—these were Quraysh converts from Mecca who had emigrated to Medina. The other group consisted of the first Muslims of

Medina. Because these Medinan Muslims provided food, shelter, and support to the recently arrived Meccans, they became known as the Helpers.

THE COVENANT

1341 Mohammed wrote up a charter or covenant for a basis of law and government. The religion of Islam now had a political system with power over those outside the mosque. All Muslims, whether from Mecca, Medina, or elsewhere, were part of a community, *umma*, that excluded others. There was one set of ethics for the Muslims and another set for the non-Muslims. Duality was established as a fundamental principle of Islamic ethics.

1341 A Muslim should oppose anyone who sowed discord among other Muslims. A Muslim should not kill another Muslim, nor should he help a non-Muslim against a Muslim. Muslims were friends to each other to the exclusion of non-Muslims. Muslims should avenge bloodshed of other Muslims in jihad. A non-believer should not intervene against a Muslim.

1342 The Jews who aligned themselves with Mohammed were to be treated fairly. Jews were to help pay for war if they fought alongside the Muslims. No Jew could go to war without the permission of Mohammed, except for revenge killings. Jews had to help Muslims if they were attacked. All trouble and controversies were to be judged by Mohammed and no Quraysh or other unbelieving Meccans were to be aided.

CALL TO PRAYER

1346 While the mosque was being built, one of the Muslim Arab leaders died. Mohammed believed the Jews and hypocrites (those who converted out of pressure but did not really believe) would say that if Mohammed was a real prophet the man would not have died. Instead of choosing a new leader for the Arab clan, Mohammed became the leader.

1347 The rule of Islam became firmly established. Taxes were established, punishments were set, and religious rules were established. There was the small problem of how to call the Muslims to prayer. The Jews used a horn; the Christians used a bell. Islam needed a different call. It was decided to use a loud chant from a high place to call the faithful to prayer.

MARRIAGE

M177 About seven months after arriving in Medina, Mohammed, in his late fifties, celebrated his marriage to Aisha, now age nine. She moved out of her father's house into what was to become a compound of apartments adjoining the mosque. She was allowed to bring her dolls into the harem due to her age; this was a big decision since Mohammed hated images. Aisha was the only virgin Mohammed ever married.

The Hadith regarding Mohammed's marriage to Aisha:

B5,58,234 *Mohammed engaged me when I [Aisha] was a girl of six years. We went to Medina; then I got ill and my hair fell down. Later on my hair grew again and my mother, Um Ruman, came to me while I was playing in a swing with some of my girl friends. She called me, and I went to her, not knowing what she wanted to do to me. She caught me by the hand and made me stand at the door of the house. I was breathless then and, when my breathing became all right, she took some water and rubbed my face and head with it.*

Then she took me into the house. There in the house I saw some Helper women who said, "Best wishes and Allah's Blessing and good luck." Then she entrusted me to them and they prepared me for the marriage. Unexpectedly Mohammed came to me in the forenoon, and my mother handed me over to him. At that time I was a girl of nine years of age.

B8,73,151 *Aisha said, "I used to play with the dolls in the presence of Mohammed, and my girl friends also used to play with me. When Mohammed used to enter my dwelling place, they used to hide themselves, but Mohammed would call them to join and play with me." The playing with the dolls and similar images is forbidden, but it was allowed for Aisha at that time, as she was a little girl, having not yet reached the age of puberty.*

M008,3311 *Aisha reported that Mohammed married her when she was seven years old, and she was taken to his house as a bride when she was nine, and her dolls were with her; and when he (Mohammed) died she was eighteen years old.*

THE JEWS AND HYPOCRITES

24:47 There are those who say, "We believe in Allah and His Messenger and we obey." But just as soon as this is said, they turn their backs. These are not the believers.

1351 After a few months the leaders of the Jews could see what lay ahead and began to speak against Mohammed. They were joined by some of the Arabs who respected the ancient religions that Mohammed condemned. Just as in Mecca, he disparaged others' religious customs, cursed their gods, and said their ancestors would burn in Hell. Most of the Arabs who disapproved of Mohammed's tactics were silent in public because of Mohammed's increasing political power. Those Muslims who were public Muslims but private critics were called *hypocrites.*

1351 The rabbis began to ask difficult questions of Mohammed, who would not tolerate any resistance to his word. Doubts and questions about his doctrine were doubts about Allah, and doubts about Allah were evil. However, two of the Jewish Arabs joined Mohammed as Muslims. They believed him when he said he was the prophesied Jewish prophet come to fulfill the Torah.

1351 Some of the Arabs pretended to convert in order to save their lives. Actually, they preferred the Jews to Mohammed and worked against Mohammed when they could.

THE HYPOCRITES

1351 Before Mohammed arrived, the Arabs who practiced the ancient Arabic religions were content within their religion and tolerant of other religions. Many Arabs became Muslims because they were pressured to do so. They chose Islam to save their lives. But in secret they were hypocrites who allied themselves with the Jews because they thought Mohammed was deluded.

According to the Koran:

> 2:8 *And some of the people [the Jews] say, "We believe in Allah and the Day," although they do not really believe.*

1365 The hypocrites were also cursed by Allah and would be damned:

2:9 *They wish to deceive Allah and His believers, but they fool no one but themselves although they do not know it. Their hearts are diseased, and Allah has increased their suffering. They will suffer an excruciating doom because of their lies.*

1365 The Koran gives an analogy about the hypocrites:

2:16 *It is these who have bought error at the price of guidance. Their purchase is profitless, and they have lost the right direction. They are like the ones who lit a fire, and when it shed its light all around them, Allah took it away and left them in total darkness where they were unable to see. Deaf, dumb and blind, they will never turn back to the right path.*

1355 One of the Medinans became a Muslim and later began to doubt the truth of Mohammed and said, "If this man is right, we are worse than donkeys." His best friend had converted and told Mohammed of this friend's doubts. Mohammed believed allegiance to Islam came before family, nation, or friend. When he confronted the man about his remarks and doubts, the man denied them.

The Koran's comments:

9:74 *They swear by Allah that they said nothing wrong, yet they spoke blasphemy, and some Muslims became unbelievers. They planned what they could not carry out [a plan against Mohammed], and only disapproved of it because Allah and His Messenger had enriched them by His bounty [the resistance to Mohammed decreased when the money from the spoils of war came into the Medinan economy]. If they repent, it will be better for them, but if they fall back into their sin, Allah will afflict them with a painful doom in this world and the next. On earth they will have neither friend nor protector.*

1356 Ironically, the friend who reported the doubts to Mohammed later turned against Mohammed, killed two Muslims during battle, and fled to Mecca. Mohammed ordered him killed, but he escaped. Again the Koran:

3:86 *How will Allah guide the people who fall into disbelief after having been believers and having acknowledged the messenger as true and after having received clear signs? Allah does not guide those that do evil. As for these, they will receive Allah's curse, as well as the curse of His angels and of all mankind, and they will live under it forever. Their punishment will not be lightened nor will they be forgiven except for those who repent and change their ways. Allah is forgiving and merciful.*

1357 Mohammed used to say one of the hypocrites had the same face as Satan. The man used to sit and listen to Mohammed and then take what he said back to the hypocrites. He said of Mohammed, "Mohammed is all ears. If anyone tells him anything he will believe it." The Koran speaks of him:

> 9:61 *There are some of them who injure the Messenger and say, "He is only a hearer." Say: He is a hearer of good for you. He believes in Allah and believes in the faithful. He is a mercy to those of you who believe, but those who injure the Messenger of Allah will suffer a painful doom.*

1357 Later at the Battle of Uhud, one of the hypocrites said that if it were left to him they would not be there. The Koran's response:

> 3:154 *Then, after the trouble Allah sent down upon you, He sent down calmness to wash over some of you. Some were overtaken by sleep, and others lay awake, stirred by their own passions, ignorantly thinking unjust thoughts about Allah. And they ask, "What do we gain by this affair?" Say: Truly the affair is entirely in Allah's hands. They hide in their hearts that which they do not want to tell you. They speak out saying, "If we had any say in this affair then none of us would have been killed here." Say: If you had stayed at home, those of you who were destined to be killed would have died regardless. This has taken place so that Allah might test your faith and see what is in your hearts.*

1357 The same man later said at another tough battle, "Mohammed has said we will take the treasures of Persia and Rome, but it is not safe for us to go to the privy." Again the Koran:

> 33:12 *There were the believers tried, and they were severely shaken. The hypocrites and the diseased of heart said, "Allah and His Messenger promised us only to deceive us."*

1358 One of the hypocrites excused his criticism by saying he was only talking and jesting. No criticism was too small to go unnoticed. The Koran:

> 2:14 *And when they meet with the faithful they say, "We believe too." But when they are alone with their fellow devils [Jews and Christians] they say, "Really, we are with you. We were only mocking them."*

1365 Mohammed said the hypocrites changed their faces depending upon whom they were with. When they were with Muslims, they believed. But when they were with the evil ones (the Jews) they said they were loyal to them. It was the Jews who ordered them to deny the truth and contradict Mohammed.

> 2:15 *Allah will throw their mockery back on them and leave them to wander alone in their blindness.*

THE JEWS

When Mohammed came to Medina about half the population was Jewish. There were three tribes of Jews and two tribes of Arabs. Almost none of the Jews had Hebrew names and had adopted Arabic culture. At the same time, many of the Arabs' religious practices contained elements of Judaism. Before Mohammed arrived, there had been bad blood and killing among the tribes. The last battle had been fought by the two Arab tribes, but all three of the Jewish tribes had joined the battle with their particular Arab allies. In addition to that tension between the two Arab tribes, there was tension between the Jews and the Arabs.

The Jews were farmers and tradesmen and lived in their own quarters, which were somewhat fortified. In general, they were better educated and more prosperous than the Arabs were. It was because of these quarrelsome tribal relationships that Mohammed was invited to Medina. But the result was further polarization, not unity. The new split was between Islam and the Arabs and Jews who resisted Islam.

THE REAL TORAH IS IN THE KORAN

A running commentary of the Sira claims that the Jews and Christians corrupted their sacred texts in order to conceal the fact that the coming of Mohammed was prophesied in their scriptures. The stories in the Koran are similar to those of the Jewish scriptures, but they have different plots and make different points. According to Islam the difference is that the real Torah (the first five books of the Jewish scriptures: Genesis, Exodus, Leviticus, Numbers, and Deuteronomy) is in the Koran. Mohammed said the scriptures of the Jews were changed to hide the fact that Islam is the true religion. According to him, the Jewish scriptures are corrupt; the Koran is perfect and contains the real stories.

1364 But the Jews did not believe Mohammed was a prophet. In turn, the Muslims believed the Jews were in error and cursed by Allah and would never find guidance and meaning. Although the rabbis said publicly that Mohammed was a liar and would receive Hell-fire as a punishment, they really knew the Koran was right and their scriptures were falsified to avoid the truth of Mohammed. They were just too proud to admit it, and by denying his prophethood they conspired against Mohammed and Islam. Since Allah determined all that happens, it was Allah who had caused them to not believe Mohammed, and they would burn in Hell for it.

2:6 *As for the unbelievers, whether you warn them or not, they will not believe. Their hearts and ears are sealed up by Allah, and their eyes are covered as well. There will be a dreadful doom awaiting them.*

1367 The Koran and Mohammed taught that Mohammed was the final prophet. His coming had been foretold in the original Torah. Allah had blessed the Jews and protected them, but now they refused to believe the final and ideal prophet. The Jews were not ignorant but deceitful, and they knew the truth of Mohammed and hid the truth with lies.

2:40 *Children of Israel! Remember the favor I have given you, and keep your covenant with Me. I will keep My covenant with you. Fear My power. Believe in what I reveal [the Koran], which confirms your Scriptures, and do not be the first to disbelieve it. Do not part with My revelations for a petty price. Fear Me alone. Do not mix up the truth with lies or knowingly hide the truth.*

1367 The Koran repeated the many favors that Allah had done for the Jews—they were the chosen people delivered from slavery under the pharaoh and given the sacred Torah but all they had ever done was sin. They had been forgiven many times by Allah, and still they were as hard as rocks and refused to believe Mohammed. They had perverted the Torah after understanding it; the Jews had gone so far as to confuse others about Mohammed. They refused to recognize Mohammed as the true prophet, and they contradicted what they knew to be the truth found in the real Torah, not the corrupted one they produced instead.

2:74 *Then your hearts were hardened like rocks, or even worse, for there are some rocks from which rivers gush forth; some are split in two and water comes out of them, and others fall down from fear of Allah. Allah is not at all unaware of your actions.*
2:75 *Can you believers then hope that the Jews will believe you even though they heard the Word of Allah and purposefully altered it after they understood its meaning?*

1369 The Jews' sins were so great that Allah had changed them into apes and pigs. Still they would not learn and refused to admit that Mohammed was their prophet. They knew fully well the truth and hid it to confuse others. Even when they told Mohammed they believed, they concealed their resistance.

2:65 *And you know those among you who sinned on the Sabbath. We said to them, "You will be transformed into despised apes."*

5:59 *Say: O, people of the Book [Jews and Christians], do you not reject us only because we believe in Allah, in what He has sent down to us, in what He has sent before us, and because most of you are wrongdoers? Say: Can I tell you of retribution worse than this that awaits them with Allah? It is for those who incurred the curse of Allah and His anger; those whom He changed into apes [Jews] and swine [Christians]; those who worship evil are in a worse place, and have gone far astray from the right path.*
5:61 *When they presented themselves to you they said, "We believe," but they came as unbelievers to you, and as unbelievers they left. Allah well knew what they concealed.*

1370 The Jews had understood the truth and then changed it to avoid admitting Mohammed was right. They had done the same thing to Moses; when some of the Jews told Moses they wished to hear Allah as he did, he had them purify themselves and he took them to Mt. Sinai. Allah did speak so that they also might hear what he commanded and prohibited. But later Moses found that they changed the Word of Allah. So the Jews were only doing to Mohammed what they had done to Moses, changing the Torah[1].

2:75 *Can you believers then hope that the Jews will believe you even though they heard the Word of Allah and purposefully altered it after they understood its meaning?*
2:79 *Wretchedness will come to those who write their own scriptures and then claim, "This is from Allah," so that they can sell it for a pitiful price. They will have a mournful fate because of what they have written and for what they have earned by their actions.*

MOHAMMED IS THE REAL JEW

1381 Christians and Jews argued with Mohammed that if he wished to be saved from Hell he would have to convert. Mohammed answered that he was the one who truly followed the religion of Abraham and he was the true Jew with the true Torah.

2:135 *They say, "Become a Christian or a Jew, and you will be rightly guided to salvation." Say: No! We follow the religion of Abraham, the upright, and he was no idol worshipper. Say: We believe in Allah and in that which has been revealed to us, and to Abraham, Ishmael, Isaac, Jacob, and the tribes, and in that given to Moses and Jesus and all other messengers by our Lord.*

---

1. This version of Moses and Mt. Sinai is found only in the Koran.

1383 Mohammed entered a Jewish school and called the Jews to Islam. One asked him, "What is your religion, Mohammed?"

"The religion of Abraham."

"But Abraham was a Jew."

"Then let the Torah judge between us." He meant the Torah of the Koran.

> 3:66 *Abraham was neither a Jew nor a Christian, but a righteous man, a Muslim, not an idol worshipper. Doubtless the ones who follow Abraham are the closest to him, along with this messenger and the believers. Allah is protector of the faithful. Some of the People of the Book try to lead you astray, but they only mislead themselves, although they may not realize it.*

1397 Three Jews came to Mohammed and said, "Do you not allege that you follow the religion of Abraham and believe in the Torah, which we have, and testify that it is the truth from Allah?" He replied, "Certainly, but you have sinned and broken the covenant contained therein and concealed what you were ordered to make plain to men. I disassociate myself from your sin." The concealment was the part of the Torah that prophesied the coming of Ahmed (Mohammed).

> 5:71 *Say: O, people of the Book [Jews and Christians], you have no ground to stand on until you observe the Law and the Gospel and that which was sent down to you from your Lord. The Book [the Koran] that was sent down from your Lord will certainly increase the rebellion and unbelief of many of them, but do not be grieved for the unbelievers.*

1399 Jews came to Mohammed and said, "Is it true that what you have brought to us is from Allah? For our part we cannot see that it is arranged as the Torah is." He replied, "You know quite well that it is from Allah. You will find it written in the Torah which you have." By this he meant the real Torah that they concealed.

> B3,48,850 *Ibn Abbas said, "O Muslims? How do you ask the people of the Scriptures, though the Koran which was revealed to His Prophet is the most recent information from Allah and you recite it, the Book that has not been distorted? Allah has revealed to you that the people of the scriptures have changed with their own hands what was revealed to them and they have said (as regards to their corrupted Scriptures): This is from Allah, in order to get some worldly benefit thereby." Ibn Abbas added: "Isn't the knowledge revealed to you sufficient to prevent you from asking them? By Allah I have never seen any one of them asking Muslims about what has been revealed to you."*

AN OMINOUS CHANGE

1381 While living in Mecca, Mohammed spoke well of the Jews, who were few in number. In Medina there were many Jews and his relations with them were tense. Until now Mohammed had led prayer in the direction of Jerusalem. Now he changed the *kiblah,* the direction of prayer, to the Kabah in Mecca. Some of the Jews asked why he changed it since he had said he followed the religion of Abraham. The Koran:

> 2:142 *The foolish ones will say, "What makes them turn from the kiblah?" Say, Both the east and the west belong to Allah. He will guide whom He likes to the right path.*

1382 Mohammed summoned the Jews to follow Islam. He made it sound attractive and warned them of Allah's punishment and vengeance. The Jews said they would follow the religion of their fathers. The Koran:

> 2:170 *When it is said to them, "Follow what Allah has revealed," they say, "No, we follow the practices of our ancestors." What? Even though their ancestors were ignorant and without guidance?*

> B4,56,662 *The Prophet said, "You will follow the wrong ways of your predecessors so completely and literally that if they should go into the hole of a mastigure, you too will go there."*
> *We said, "O Allah's Apostle! Do you mean the Jews and the Christians?" He replied, "Whom else?"*

> B4,56,668 *Allah's Apostle said, "The Jews and the Christians do not dye their gray hair, so you shall do the opposite of what they do (i.e., they were to dye their gray hair and beards)."*

> B4,55,609 *When the Prophet came to Medina, he found the Jews fasting on the day of Ashura. They used to say: "This is a great day on which Allah saved Moses and drowned the folk of Pharaoh. Moses observed the fast on this day as a sign of gratitude to Allah."*
> *The Prophet said, "I am closer to Moses than they." So he observed the fast on that day and ordered the Muslims to fast on it.*

THE CHRISTIANS

CHAPTER 10

24:52 It is such as obey Allah and His Apostle, and fear
Allah and do right, that will win (in the end).

1401 Some Christians visited Mohammed in Medina. On the way there, one of the bishops said Mohammed was the one whom Christian scripture prophesied[1]. When another Christian asked why the bishop did not convert, he replied that he was making too much money in his Christian role. If he converted, he would lose his rank and wealth. At this time there were only about 250 Muslims in the world, and they were very poor and lived in one town in Arabia.

1404 While the Christians were in Medina, they argued religion with Mohammed. They held forth with the doctrine of the Trinity—God, Christ, and the Holy Spirit—and the divinity of Christ. Mohammed later laid out the Islamic doctrine of Christ. (*Ed.* The Koran regards the Trinity of the Christians to be Allah, Jesus, and Mary.)

1406 The Muslims believed no one had power except through Allah. Allah had given Jesus the power of raising the dead, healing the sick, and making birds of clay and having them fly away. Allah gave Jesus these signs as a manifestation of his being a prophet. But Allah did not give prophets the powers of appointing kings or the ability to change night to day. This lack of power showed that Jesus was a man, not part of a Holy Trinity. If he had been part of God, then all powers would have been in his command and he would not have had to be under the dominion of kings.

> 3:26 *Say: Allah! Lord of heaven and earth, you give power to whom you choose and take it away from whom you chose. You lift up whom you choose and You bring down whom you choose. All that is good lies within your hand. You have power to do all things.*

1407 Christ spoke in the cradle; speaking from the cradle was a sign that he was a prophet.

1408 Christ confirmed his prophethood by making clay birds fly. Through Allah, Christ healed the blind and the lepers and raised the dead.

---

1. These Christian scriptures are unknown to us.

3:49 *He will be sent out as a messenger to the Children of Israel saying, "I have come to you with a sign from your Lord. I will make a figure of a bird out of clay and then, by Allah's will, I will breathe life into it. By Allah's permission I cause the blind to see, heal the lepers, and bring the dead back to life. I will tell you what you should eat and what you should store up in your houses. This will be a sign for those who truly believe."*

1408 Mohammed taught that Christ came only through Allah. His signs of being a prophet came only from Allah. Jesus enjoined others to worship Allah, not him. But people refused to hear him, and the disciples came forth to help him with his mission. The disciples were servants of Allah and Muslims like Christ.

3:50 *"I have come to fulfill the Law which came before me and to give you permission to do certain things which were once unlawful. I come to you with a sign from your Lord, so fear Allah and obey me. Allah is my Lord and yours, so worship Him. That is the right path."*

3:52 *When Jesus saw that they did not believe, he said, "Who will be my helpers for Allah?" The disciples replied, "We will be Allah's helpers! We believe in Allah and witness our submission to Him. Lord! We believe in what you have revealed and we follow Your messenger; therefore, record us as Your witnesses."*

4:171 *People of the Book [Christians]! Do not overstep the boundaries of your religion and speak only what is true about Allah. The Messiah, Jesus, the son of Mary, is only Allah's messenger and his Word which he sent into Mary was a spirit from Him. Therefore, believe in Allah and His messengers and do not say, "Trinity." Hold back and it will be better for you. Allah is only one God. Far be it from Allah to have a son! All in the heavens and earth are His.*

5:17 *Surely they are unbelievers who say, "Allah is the Messiah, son of Mary." Say: Who has any power against Allah if He chose to destroy the Messiah, son of Mary, his mother, and all who are on the earth together? Allah's is the sovereignty of the heavens and of the earth and of all that is between them. He creates what He will, and Allah has power over all things.*

5:76 *They surely blaspheme who say, "Allah is the third of three [the Trinity]," for there is no god except one Allah, and if they do not refrain from what they say, a grievous penalty will fall on those who disbelieve.*

1409 Mohammed and the Muslims believed Christ was not crucified. When the Jews plotted against Christ, they found Allah to be the better plotter. (The Koran says more than once that Allah was better at plotting than those who plotted against Islam.) Allah took Jesus up directly to him and would refute those who said he was crucified and resurrected. On the final day, the Day of Resurrection, those who followed Christ but did not believe in his divinity would be blessed. Those who insisted Christ was God and part of the Trinity and rejected true faith would be punished in Hell.

3:54 *So the Jews plotted and Allah plotted, but Allah is the best plotter there is. And Allah said, "Jesus! I am going to end your life on earth and lift you up to Me. [Jesus did not die in the Crucifixion. He was taken to Allah. He will return to kill the anti-Christ and then die a natural death.] I will send the unbelievers away from you and lift up those who believe above all others until the Day of Resurrection. Then all will return to Me and I will judge their disputes. As for the unbelievers, they will be punished with excruciating agony in this world and the world to come. They will have no one to help them.*

4:156 *They said, "We killed the Messiah, Jesus the son of Mary, Allah's messenger." But they did not kill him or crucify him, although it appeared so to them [the person crucified was not Jesus, but a "double"]. And those who argued about it were in doubt concerning him. They had no clear knowledge about him and only went with opinion. They did not really kill him, but Allah lifted him up to Himself. Allah is mighty and wise!*

JIHAD, WAR AGAINST ALL

CHAPTER 11

*4:59 Believers! Obey Allah and obey His Messenger
and those among you with authority. If you have a
disagreement about anything, refer it to Allah and His
Messenger if you believe in Allah and the Last Day.
This is the best and fairest way to settle a dispute.*

In Mecca, Mohammed had divided the community into followers of
Islam and followers of the native Arabic religions. He adopted all the clas-
sical Jewish stories to prove his prophecy and spoke well of the Jews. But
there were few Jews living there, and no one argued with him.

Upon coming to Medina, where half the residents were Jews, Mohammed divided the community into thirds: Islam, the Jews and their allies,
and those who practiced the native Arabic religions. He made a sharp division between Islam and Christianity as well.

I415 Mohammed then prepared for war as commanded by Allah. He
would fight his enemies, those who were not Muslims. This was thirteen
years after he started preaching, about one to two years after leaving Mecca and going to Medina.

> 3:151 *Soon shall We cast terror into the hearts of the unbelievers, for that
> they joined companions with Allah, for which He had sent no authority:
> Their abode will be the Fire: And evil is the home of the wrongdoers!*

THE FIRST RAID

I416 At age 53, Mohammed sent forth his fighters to Waddan in search
of the Quraysh. They returned without fighting.

THE EXPEDITION OF UBAYDA

I416 Mohammed sent out Ubayda on an expedition with sixty to eighty
riders, and they encountered a large number of Quraysh. No fighting took
place, but Islam shot the first arrow. It was shot by Sad.

The Arabs had a tradition of war poetry. This poem was written in that
tradition:

They (the Quraysh) howled like bitches driven back
to their lairs.
If they follow the religion of their fathers
Allah's punishment on them will not tarry.
A valiant band will descend upon them
And leave their women without husbands. —Abu Bakr

HAMZA'S EXPEDITION

I419 Mohammed sent Hamza out with thirty riders, and they met three hundred riders from Mecca. They separated without a fight.

THE RAID ON BUWAT

I421 Mohammed sent men out looking for Quraysh. No contact was made.

THE RAID ON AL-USHAYRA

I421 This time Mohammed led the raid. They left Medina looking for Quraysh but made no contact.

THE RAID OF SAD

I423 Sad set out with eight men on a raid but made no contact with the enemy, the Quraysh.

THE RAID ON SAFAWAN

I423 After Mohammed came back from his raid, one of the Quraysh raided Medina and stole some camels. Mohammed and some men set out to catch him but made no contact.

Until now, armed men had been sent out to kill and take the spoils of war and prisoners but without success. After seven attempts, Islam was finally able to destroy the enemies of Mohammed and Allah.

JIHAD—THE FIRST KILLING

I423 Mohammed sent Abdullah out with eight men. He gave him a letter and asked him not to read it for two days. Abdullah agreed. The letter told him where to go and wait for the Quraysh. While camping, two of his men lost their camel and stayed behind to look for it while the rest of the men went on.

1424 A Quraysh caravan loaded with leather and raisins came upon the band of Muslims. When the Quraysh saw them they were scared because they had slept not very far away. But one of the Muslims had a shaved head, which was a mark of a religious pilgrim, so the Quraysh felt better. They were safe. The native religions had sacred months in which violence was forbidden to all. This was a sacred month, and they were unarmed.

1425 The Muslims took council. They were faced with a dilemma: if they attacked the caravan now, they would be killing in a sacred month. Luckily, the sacred month ended that day and the next day there would be no taboo about killing. But there was another problem: by nightfall they would be in the sacred area of Mecca. In the sanctified area, there could never be any killing. They hesitated and talked about what to do. They decided to kill as many as possible and take their goods before the next day.

1425 Islam drew first blood against the Quraysh of Mecca. They attacked the unarmed men. Amr, the first man to be killed by jihad, was shot by an arrow. One man escaped, and they captured two others. The Muslims took the enemies' camels with their goods and headed back to Medina and Mohammed. On the way they talked about how Mohammed would get one fifth of the stolen goods.

1425 When they got back, Mohammed said he had not ordered them to attack in the sacred month. He detained the caravan and the two prisoners and refused to do anything with them or the goods. The prisoners said, "Mohammed has violated the sacred month, shed blood therein, stolen goods, and taken prisoners."

But the Koran said:

> 2:217 *When they ask you about fighting in the holy month, say: Fighting at this time is a serious offense, but it is worse in Allah's eyes to deny others the path to Him, to disbelieve in Him, and to drive His worshippers out of the Sacred Mosque. Idolatry is a greater sin than murder. They will not stop fighting you until you turn away from your religion. But any of you who renounce your faith and die an unbeliever will have your works count for nothing in this world and the world to come. These people will be prisoners of the Fire, where they will live forever.*

1426 According to Mohammed, to resist the doctrine of Islam and persuade Muslims to drop their faith was worse than killing. Before Islam, the rule of justice in Arabia was a killing for a killing, but now to resist Islam was worse than murder. Those who argued against Islam and resisted Islam could be killed as a sacred act. So the murder and theft were sanctified. The spoils of war were distributed and a ransom was set for the prisoners. The men who had killed and stolen were now concerned about whether they would get their share of the spoils. So once again the Koran spoke:

> 2:218 *Those who believe and those who have fled their countries and have fought for Allah's cause [jihad] may hope for His mercy; Allah is forgiving and merciful.*

1426 As Muslims who had been exiled and fought they were blessed by Allah. They received their spoils of war and Mohammed took his 20 percent.

> B4,53,351 *Allah's Apostle said, "The spoils of war have been made legal for me."*

Another war poem:

> *You [Quraysh] count war in the holy month a grave matter*
> *But graver is your opposition to Mohammed and your unbelief.*
> *Though you defame us for killing Amr*
> *Our lances drank Amr's blood.*
> *We lit the flame of war. —Abu Bakr*

THE BATTLE THAT CHANGED THE WORLD

CHAPTER 12

*4:42 On that day, the unbelievers and those who disobeyed
the Messenger will wish they could sink into the earth
for they cannot hide a single thing from Allah.*

FIGHTING IN ALLAH'S CAUSE—BADR

I428 Mohammed heard from spies that Abu Sufyan, the chief of the Quraysh, was coming from Syria with a large caravan and thirty or forty men. Mohammed called the Muslims together and said, "Go out and attack it, and perhaps Allah will give us the prey." Many were eager, but others were reluctant. Some of the Quraysh were their relatives and they did not want to fight and kill them.

I428 As the caravan approached Medina, Abu Sufyan became worried and questioned every rider on the road about Mohammed. Then he was informed that indeed Mohammed was going to attack. He sent out a fast rider to Mecca for aid. When the rider entered Mecca, he called out, "Oh Quraysh, the caravan! Mohammed and his companions are lying in wait to steal your property. Help! Help!"

I430 The Quraysh said this raid would not be as easy as killing an unarmed man. The leaders and their men saddled up and prepared to protect what was theirs, but as they prepared for war they remembered an old score with an enemy clan. The quarrel had never been settled. Would their enemies attack Mecca while they were away? One of the chiefs of the enemy clan said they would not attack and the Quraysh left with haste.

I433 Mohammed and his men headed out of Medina for what was to prove one of the most important battles in all of history, a battle that would change the world forever. The party had seventy camels and about three hundred men. On the way they met a nomad and asked if he had seen the Quraysh. He had not. Then the men told him to salute the prophet of Allah. The nomad said, "Well, if he is a prophet, can he tell me what was in the womb of my she-camel?" One of Mohammed's men replied, "Don't question Mohammed, but I can tell you what is in the womb of your camel. It is a goat from the last time you had sex with her." They went on their way but no wiser.

1434 News came to Mohammed that the Quraysh had set out from Mecca with armed men to defend their property. He stopped and held a strategy meeting. The Meccan Immigrants said they would go wherever Mohammed told them to go and do whatever he asked. The leader of the Helpers said although their treaty with Mohammed covered only the defense of Medina they would fight for him for any reason, at any place, and at any time. "We believe in you. We hear and we will obey. By Allah, if you asked us to plunge into the sea we would do so to the last man. We do not fear the enemy. We are experienced warriors and trustworthy in combat."

1435 Mohammed was cheered. He said, "I see the enemy dead on the ground. Allah has promised me either the caravan or their army." They headed toward Badr and camped near there for the night. Mohammed sent several scouts to the well at Badr, where they found two black slaves with water camels. The scouts felt sure they were from the Quraysh caravan and brought back them back to Mohammed. Two of Mohammed's men questioned them as Mohammed prayed nearby. The men replied that they were from the Quraysh army. Mohammed's men began to beat and torture the slaves as Mohammed continued praying. Then the slaves said they were from Abu Sufyan's caravan and the men stopped beating them.

1436 Mohammed told his men that the slaves had been truthful until they started to beat and torture them. Then the slaves had lied, but it had been the lie their captors wanted to hear. "By Allah, you beat them when they tell the truth and leave them alone when they lie." Mohammed then took over the interrogation and asked the men how many of the Quraysh there were. They did not know. He then asked how many camels they killed each day for food and was told nine or ten. That meant there were nine hundred to a thousand Quraysh fighters. He then asked who the leaders of the Quraysh were, and they told him. Mohammed was delighted and told his warriors that Mecca had sent their best men to be slaughtered.

1437 Two other scouts had obtained information from two village girls that the caravan would arrive the following day.

1437 Abu Sufyan rode ahead of his caravan and met one of his own scouts at the well. He asked if they had seen anything to cause concern, and they told him they had seen only two riders on the hill above. Sufyan rode to the top of the hill, dismounted, and examined the camel dung there. He crumbled the dung in his hands and saw a certain type of date seeds. Medina! The camels were from Medina. Mohammed's scouts had been there! He hurried back and directed the caravan away from Badr.

1438 Abu Sufyan had saved the caravan, and now he went to the armed band of the Quraysh who had come out to protect it. He told them the caravan was safe and they could return home. But the band's leader, Abu Jahl, said they were now near Badr and it was a time for a fair, and to the fair they would go. They would feast and drink and the Arabs would respect them for not running away from Mohammed. Two of the clans who were allied with the Quraysh wanted no part of such a useless display and bowed out and returned to Mecca.

1439 Each army had an idea of the location of the other. Mohammed went ahead to choose a place to camp and set up for battle on the morrow. One of his men asked if the choice were by Allah or if Mohammed made a personal choice. It was a personal choice. His man then suggested they choose a spot at the well farthest from the area where the Quraysh would camp and plug the wells between them and the Quraysh. That way, the next day they would have water and the Quraysh would have none. Mohammed agreed and put men to the task. Islam would have water and the non-Muslims would be dry.

1440 The Quraysh marched forth at daybreak. Mohammed watched as they came down the hill into the valley. They stopped at the bottom and sent out a scout. While the scout was gone, the Quraysh began to talk among themselves. Some argued not to fight because half the Muslims were from Mecca and kin. One man had a dream that portended ill for the Quraysh. Morale was sinking but one of the Quraysh rallied them with the memory of Amr whom the Muslims had killed even though he was Quraysh.

1440 As Mohammed saw the Quraysh march into the small valley, he said, "O Allah, here come the Quraysh, in their vanity and pride, contending with you and calling me a liar. O Allah, give me the help you promised. Destroy them this morning!"

1443 One of the Quraysh had a hot temper and decided on his own that he would drink from the well in front of the Muslims. Off he went to be met by Islam's finest and strongest man, Hamza. In one blow Hamza's sword cut through the man's leg at the shin. He fell on his back with his leg pointed toward his companions, gushing blood. The man then started to crawl to the well. Hamza killed him by sword before he could reach the well. Islam drew first blood, and the killing was a bad omen for the Quraysh.

1443 Three of the Muslims stepped forth from their ranks to engage in single-handed combat with three of the Quraysh. One of the Quraysh yelled for them to identify themselves. The Muslims gave their names, and the Quraysh replied, "O Mohammed, send forth some warriors who are peers of ours; we are nobles. Don't send peasants to fight with nobility." Mohammed sent forth three new men. They identified themselves, and the Quraysh said, "Yes, these are nobles and our peers."

I443 The men went at each other with swords. Two of the Muslims, Ali and Hamza, quickly killed their opponents. The other Muslim and Quraysh wounded each other and Ali and Hamza quickly killed the Quraysh. They took their mortally wounded comrade back to Mohammed. The dying Muslim asked Mohammed if he was a martyr. "Indeed, you are," replied Mohammed.

> B4,53,352 *Allah's Apostle said, "Allah guarantees him who strives in His Cause, and whose motivation for going out is nothing but jihad in His Cause and belief in His Word, that He will admit him into Paradise, if martyred, or bring him back to his dwelling place, whence he has come out, with what he gains of reward and spoils of war."*

I445 Some arrows flew and one Muslim was killed. Mohammed addressed his army. "By Allah, every man who is slain this day by fighting with courage and advancing, not retreating, will enter Paradise." One of his men who had been eating dates said, "You mean there is nothing between me and Paradise except being killed by the Quraysh?" He flung the dates to the side, picked up his sword, and set out to fight. He got his wish and was later killed.

I445 One of Mohammed's men asked what made Allah laugh. Mohammed answered, "When a warrior plunges into the midst of the enemy without armor." The man removed his coat of mail, picked up his sword, and made ready to attack.

I445 It was time for the two armies to close ranks and move forward. Mohammed had said his warriors were not to start until he gave the order. Now he took a handful of pebbles and threw them at the Quraysh and said, "Curse those faces." The Muslims advanced. The battle had begun.

> B4,59,333 *Az-Zubair said, "I met Ubaida Bin Said Bin Al-As on the day of the Battle of Badr, and he was covered with armor, so much that only his eyes were visible. He was surnamed Abu-Al-Karish. He said proudly, 'I am Abu-Al-Karish.'*
>
> *"I attacked him with the spear and pierced his eye and he died. I put my foot over his body to pull that spear out, but even then I had to use a great force to take it out as its both ends were bent."*
>
> *Urwa said, "Later on, Allah's Apostle asked Az-Zubair for the spear, and he gave it to him. When Allah's Apostle died,*

Az-Zubair took it back. After that Abu Bakr demanded it, and he gave it to him, and when Abu Bakr died, Az-Zubair took it back. Umar then demanded it from him, and he gave it to him. When Umar died, Az-Zubair took it back, and then Uthman demanded it from him, and he gave it to him. When Uthman was martyred, the spear remained with Ali's offspring. Then Abdullah Bin Az-Zubair demanded it back, and it remained with him till he was martyred."

1446 Mohammed had issued orders that his uncle, Al Abbas, who had defended Mohammed in Mecca, was not to be killed. One of the Muslims said, "We are to kill our own relatives while we save Al Abbas? By Allah, if I meet him I will sink my sword into his flesh."

1446 When Mohammed heard a report of this he said to Umar, "Should the face of the uncle of a prophet be marked with the sword?" Umar said, "Let me cut off the head of the man who said that! He is a false Muslim." The Muslim who had made the remark said, "I never felt safe after that."

1446 While the battle was raging, one of the Muslims approached Al Abbas and told him of his security. He asked if his friends would be saved as well. "No, we will not spare any of your friends." He replied, "In that case I will die with them. The women of Mecca will not say that I saved myself and forsook his friends." He then said:

A son of the Free betrays not his friend
Till he is dead, or sees him safe on his way. —Al Abbas

He was killed.

1446 As the battle was ending and the prisoners were being rounded up, Mohammed saw a look of disgust on Sad's face. He said, "You seem to dislike what you see." Sad replied, "Yes, by Allah, this is our first defeat of the unbelievers and we should slaughter them all to the last man."

1451 As the battle wound down, Mohammed issued orders for the fighters to be on the lookout for Abu Jahl, the enemy of Allah, among the slain. He was found still fighting in a thicket. When a Muslim fighter got to within striking distance of Abu Jahl, the Muslim made for him and cut off his lower leg and sent it flying. It flew like a date stone flying from the pestle in a date mill. Another Muslim passed as Abu Jahl lay dying and put his foot on his neck. The Muslim said, "Has Allah put you to shame, enemy of Allah?" Abu Jahl gasped, "How has He shamed me? Am I any more remarkable than any other you have killed?" The Muslim cut off his head.

1452 He took the head back to Mohammed and said, "Here is the head of the enemy of Allah," and threw it at Mohammed's feet. The prophet said, "Praise be to Allah."

> B4,53,369 *At the Battle of Badr, I [Abdur-Rahman] stood in the front line between two young boys and wished that I had been the stronger man. One of them got my attention and said, "Uncle, do you know Abu Jahl?"*
>
> *I said, "Yes, why do you ask?"*
>
> *He replied, "People tell me he speaks ill of Mohammed. By Allah, if I see him, I will not break off my attack until one of us is dead."*
>
> *I was shocked to hear this. Then the other boy said to me the same thing. Sometime later, I saw Abu Jahl and I pointed him out to the boys, saying, "There is the man you seek."*
>
> *After ferociously attacking and killing him, the boys went to Mohammed and told him of Abu Jahl's death.*
>
> *Mohammed asked, "Who killed him?" They both truthfully said, "I have killed him."*
>
> *Mohammed asked, "Did you clean your swords?"*
>
> *They answered, "No."*
>
> *Mohammed glanced at their swords and said, "Obviously, you both killed him, so his possessions will be divided between the two of you."*

1455 As the bodies were dragged to the well, one of the Muslims saw the body of his father thrown in. He said, "My father was a virtuous, wise, kind, and cultured man. I had hoped he would become a Muslim, but he died an unbeliever. His abode is Hell-fire forever." Before Islam, killing of kin and tribal brothers had been forbidden since the dawn of time. After Islam, brother would kill brother and sons would kill fathers fighting in Allah's cause: Jihad.

1454 The bodies of the Quraysh were thrown into a well. The Apostle of Allah leaned over the well and shouted at the bodies, "O people of the well, have you found what Allah promised to be true?" The Muslims were puzzled by his question. "Are you speaking to dead people?" they asked. Mohammed explained that the dead could understand him.

1454 In the middle of the night Mohammed's companions heard him say, "O people of the well. Have you found what my lord promised me to be true? You were evil kinsfolk to your prophet. You called me a liar when others believed me. You cast me out when others took me in. You fought against me when others fought alongside me. Have you found what your Lord promised you to be true?"

1456 Now it was time to take the property from the dead who could no longer claim what was theirs. It was now the spoils of jihad and the profit of Islam. As the spoils of war piled up the Muslims began to quarrel over who got what for profit. Those who were on the front lines argued that they did the killing; therefore, the goods were theirs. Those who stayed behind to guard Mohammed said they had equal right. Mohammed confiscated the whole trove. He then divided it equally among all who were there. He took one fifth for himself.

> B4,53,359 *Uthman did not join the Badr battle because he was married to one of the daughters of Allah's Apostle, and she was ill. So, the Prophet said to him, "You will get a reward and a share from the spoils of war similar to the reward and the share of one who has taken part in the Badr battle."*

Those who survived the battle became rich through the spoils of war. The dead were martyrs and had the best reward.

> B4,52,64 *Um Ar-Rubai bint Al-Bara came to the Prophet and said, "O Allah's Prophet! Will you tell me about Hartha?"*
> *Hartha had been killed [i.e., martyred] on the day of Badr with an arrow thrown by an unidentified person.*
> *She added, "If he is in Paradise, I will be patient; otherwise, I will weep bitterly for him."*
> *Mohammed said, "O mother of Hartha! There are Gardens in Paradise and your son got the best place in Paradise."*

There was one prisoner from Mecca whom Mohammed knew well. He knew the stories of the Greeks and Persians. When Mohammed had told his stories of the Jews and Arabs, he had told the stories of the Greeks and Persians and said he was the better story-teller. It was Al Nadr.

1459 They set off for Medina with the treasure of war and the prisoners to be ransomed, except for Al Nadr. Mohammed had a grudge against him and ordered him killed. Before the sword struck, Al Nadr asked, "Who will care for my family?"

M230 The prophet replied, "Hell!" After he fell dead, Mohammed said, "Unbeliever in Allah and His prophet and His book! I give thanks to Allah who has killed you and made my eyes satisfied."

1462 A survivor took the news of the disaster to the Meccans. One of the chiefs ordered that there be no wailing or public mourning so the Muslims could draw no pleasure from their loss. They also decided to be slow to pay the ransom to Mohammed for the captured Meccans in order to help lower the ransom price.

1464 An old Muslim had gone from Medina to Mecca on a pilgrimage and wound up in Mecca after the loss. He was made a prisoner and used in exchange for one of the Meccans.

A POSSIBLE NEW WIFE

1461 When Mohammed saw Ummul Fadl she was a crawling baby and he said, "If she grows up and I am still alive, I will marry her." At this time he was about 55.

THE KORAN—WAR TREASURE

CHAPTER 13

4:69 Those who obey Allah and His Messenger will live
with the messengers and the saints and the martyrs
and the righteous. What wonderful company!

1476 After the Battle of Badr, an entire sura (chapter) of the Koran was added. The eighth chapter is called "War Treasure," or "Booty," and also the "Spoils of War." The idea of the Battle of Badr was entirely Mohammed's. Many of the Muslims had no desire to go to war.

> 8:5 *Remember how your Lord commanded you to leave your homes to fight for the truth, but some of the believers were opposed to it? They disputed the truth after you had revealed it, as if they were being led to certain death before their eyes.*

1476 The armed Muslims had wanted to attack the caravan, not the army.

> 8:7 *And when Allah promised that you would defeat one of the two groups of enemies, you wished to attack the group that was defenseless. But Allah wished to justify the truth of His words and to cut the unbelievers down so that the truth would triumph and the lies would be shown false, much to the opposition of the guilty.*

1477 The Muslims had not fought by themselves. Allah had sent a thousand angels to help kill those who worshiped in the ancient ways and rituals. To resist Mohammed was a death sentence from Allah.

> 8:12 *Then your Lord spoke to His angels and said, "I will be with you. Give strength to the believers. I will send terror into the unbelievers' hearts, cut off their heads and even the tips of their fingers!" This was because they opposed Allah and His messenger. Ones who oppose Allah and His messenger will be severely punished by Allah. We said, "This is for you! Taste it and know that the unbelievers will receive the torment of the Fire."*

There were other rules of war, such as the following:

1477 When a Muslim met a non-Muslim in war, he was not to turn his back except as a tactical maneuver. A Muslim fighting in Allah's cause had to face the enemy. Not doing so brought on the wrath of Allah and the judgment of Hell. Fear was not an option for a jihadist.

8:15 *Believers! When you meet the unbelievers marching into battle, do not turn your back to them to retreat. Anyone who turns his back on them, unless it is for a tactical advantage or to join another company, will incur Allah's wrath and Hell will be his home, truly a tortuous end.*

1478 When Mohammed spoke, a Muslim had only one choice: Listen and obey.

8:20 *Believers! Be obedient to Allah and His messenger, and do not turn your backs now that you know the truth. Do not be like the ones who say, "We hear," but do not obey. The vilest creatures in Allah's sight are the ones who are deaf, dumb, and without sense.*

1480 If those who practiced the old religions submitted to Islam, all would be forgiven. But if not, they were to take a lesson from Badr. The jihad would not stop until non-Muslims surrendered to Islam. Only submission to Islam would save the non-Muslim.

8:38 *Tell the unbelievers that if they change their ways, then they will be forgiven for their past. If, however, they continue to sin, let them remember the fate of those who came before them. Fight against them until they stop persecuting you, and Allah's religion reigns sovereign over all others. If they cease, Allah knows all they do, but if they turn their backs, know that Allah is your protector—an excellent helper.*

1481 After war and victory there were treasure and spoils of war. One fifth was to go to the apostle, Allah's prophet.

8:41 *Know that a fifth of all your spoils of war [the traditional cut for the leader was a fourth] belongs to Allah, to His messenger, to the messenger's family, the orphans, and needy travelers. Sincerely believe in Allah and in what was sent down to you through His messenger on the day of victory when the two armies met. Allah is powerful over all things.*

1482 In war (jihad) the warriors were to remember Allah all the time and they would prevail. They were to obey Mohammed and not argue with him or each other. Don't quit, they were told, and don't lose morale. Allah would see that they prevailed.

8:45 *Believers! When you confront their army stand fast and pray to Allah without ceasing so that you will be victorious. Obey Allah and His messenger, and do not argue with one another for fear that you will lose courage and strength. Be patient for Allah is with the patient.*

1482 Death was just the beginning of the unbelievers' troubles. Allah would use his angels to torture them forever.

8:50 *If only you could witness the angels carrying off the unbelievers' souls! They slash their faces and backs, saying, "Taste the torment of the Fire!"*

1483 Mohammed was to encourage war and lead the believers to war. With Allah's help, twenty Muslims could kill two hundred non-Muslims, and a hundred Muslims could destroy a thousand. The unbelievers were ignorant and easily defeated by jihad.

8:65 *Messenger! Call the faithful to fight. If there are among you twenty who will stand fast, they will overcome two hundred; and if there are a hundred of you, they will overcome a thousand unbelievers for they lack understanding.*

1484 Sad had been right about taking prisoners after the battle: Take no prisoners until Islam has made all submit. They were to forget the ransom and the money, Mohammed said, because submission of the non-believers was all that mattered.

8:67 *A prophet should not take prisoners of war until he has fought and slaughtered in the land. You desire the bounty of the world, but Allah desires the bounty for you of the world to come. Allah is mighty and wise.*

> B1,7,331 *The Prophet said, "I have been given five things which were not given to anyone else before me.*
> 1. *Allah made me victorious by awe, by His frightening my enemies for a distance of one month's journey.*
> 2. *The earth has been made for me and for my followers a place for praying and to perform my rituals; therefore, anyone of my followers can pray whenever the time of a prayer is due.*
> 3. *The spoils of war have been made lawful for me yet they were not lawful for anyone else before me.*
> 4. *I have been given the right of intercession on the Day of Resurrection.*
> 5. *Every Prophet was sent to his nation but only I have been sent to all mankind."*

1484 Mohammed was now a political force unlike any ever seen in history. The fusion of religion and politics with a universal mandate created a permanent force. To this day, the mandate continues. There will be no peace until all the world is Islam. The treasure of war, the spoils, will provide the wealth of Islam. The awe of Mohammed is the fear of Allah.

Mohammed left Mecca as a preacher and prophet. He entered Medina with about 150 Muslim converts. After a year in Medina there were 250 to 300 Muslims and most of them were very poor. After the Battle of Badr, a new Islam emerged. Mohammed rode out of Medina as a politician and a general. Islam became an armed political force with a religious motivation, jihad. After Badr, the Muslims were prosperous and they gained in power.

I518 A poem by Ali:

> *Have you not seen how Allah favored Mohammed?*
> *How he brought humiliation on the unbelievers?*
> *Who were put to shame in death and captivity,*
> *While the Apostle of Allah's victory was glorious.*
> *Being sent by Allah in righteousness,*
> *He brought the Koran down from Allah.*
> *Dead in Badr's well lay many,*
> *Error called them and they responded.*
> *Now they are in Hell,*
> *Too occupied to rage furiously against us.*

CONTINUED JIHAD

CHAPTER 14

*4:115 Anyone who opposes the Messenger after having
received Our guidance and follows a path other than
that of the true believer will be left to his own devices.
We will lead him into Hell, an evil home.*

THE RAID ON THE TRIBE OF B. SULAYM

I540 Seven days after Mohammed returned from Badr he led an armed
force in a raid against a tribe allied with the Quraysh. The fighting band
waited for three days at a watering hole but found no opportunity for killing and returned to Medina.

THE RAID OF THE PARCHED GRAIN

I543 Abu Sufyan wanted revenge on Mohammed for his defeat at Badr,
and he swore that he would not have sex[1] until he got it. He headed out
with two hundred men to fulfil his vow. After a short day's ride, he stopped
near Medina at night and got information about the Muslims. The next
morning his army burned some new palm date trees, killed two Muslims,
and left. The Muslims gave hot pursuit. Along the trail they found some
sacks of parched grain that Abu Sufyan had abandoned to allow a fast
escape. They were not able to engage Abu Sufyan and finally returned to
Medina.

THE RAID OF DHU AMARR

T1365 After the raid of parched grain, Mohammed stayed in Medina about a month. Then he raided Najd. There he stayed for a month
but never engaged any of the Quraysh or their allies, so he returned
to Medina.

---

1.   Actually what he said was that he would not practice ablution. The Arabs
considered that sex spiritually contaminated a person and a ritual cleansing
was necessary after sex. Islam fully adopted this native Arab religious practice.
Almost every aspect of religious ritual in Islam came from the native tribal
customs.

THE RAID OF BAHRAN

T1365 Mohammed and his men then set out for Bahran to seek the Quraysh. Two months later they returned to Medina without any contact with the enemies of Allah.

THE AFFAIR OF THE JEWS OF QURAYZAH

I545 There were three tribes of Jews in Medina. The Banu Qurayzah were goldsmiths and lived in a stronghold. Mohammed said they had broken the treaty signed when Mohammed came to Medina. How they did this is unclear.

I545 Mohammed assembled the Jews in their market and said, "O Jews, be careful that Allah does not bring vengeance upon you the way he did to the Quraysh. Become Muslims. You know that I am the prophet that was sent to you. You will find that in your scriptures."

I545 They replied, "O Mohammed, you seem to think that we are your people. Don't fool yourself. You may have killed a few merchants of the Quraysh, but we are men of war and real men."

I545 The response of the Koran:

> 3:12 *Say to the unbelievers, "Soon you will be defeated and thrown into Hell, a wretched home!" Truly, there has been a sign for you in the two armies which met in battle. One army fought for Allah's cause, and the other army was a group of unbelievers, and the unbelievers saw with their own eyes that their enemy was twice its actual size. Allah gives help to whom He pleases. Certainly there is a lesson to be learned in this for those who recognize it.*

I546 A little later, Mohammed besieged the Jewish tribe of Banu Qurayzah in their quarters. Neither of the other two Jewish tribes came to their support. Finally, the Jews surrendered and expected to be slaughtered after their capture.

I546 An Arab ally, bound to them by a client relationship, approached Mohammed and said, "O Mohammed, deal kindly with my clients." Mohammed ignored him. The ally repeated the request and Mohammed still ignored him. The ally grabbed Mohammed by the robe and enraged Mohammed, who said, "Let me go!" The ally said, "No, you must deal kindly with my clients. They have protected me and now you would kill them all? I fear these changes." The response by the Koran:

> 5:57 *O, you who believe, do not take those who have received the Scriptures [Jews and Christians] before you, who have scoffed and jested at your religion, or who are unbelievers for your friends. Fear Allah if you*

*are true believers. When you call to prayer, they make it a mockery and a
joke. This is because they are a people who do not understand.*

Mohammed released the Jews he had captured but took all of their
wealth and goods. He drove the first of the three tribes of Jews from Medina with only the clothes on their backs. Two tribes were left.

THE RAID OF AL QARADA

1547 Mohammed's victory at Badr and ongoing jihad caused the
Quraysh to travel by a different route to Syria. They hired a new guide to
take them over the new route. Mohammed had information about their
route and sent a party to raid them. They were carrying a great deal of silver when the caravan stopped at a watering hole. The Muslims surprised
them and the Quraysh managed to escape, but Mohammed's men stole all
the caravan's goods, including the silver. The stolen goods were delivered
to Mohammed in Medina.

THE ASSASSINATION OF AL ASHRAF, THE JEW

1548 When Al Ashraf, a Jew of Medina, heard that two of his friends of
the Quraysh had been killed at Badr, he said that being in the grave was
better than being on earth with Mohammed. To oppose Mohammed was
to be "the enemy of Allah." So the "enemy of Allah" composed some poems bewailing the loss of his friends and attacking Islam.

1551 When Mohammed heard Al Ashraf's criticism of his politics, he
said, "Who will rid me of Al Ashraf?" A Muslim said, "I will kill him for
you." Days later Mohammed found out that his assassin was not doing
anything, including eating or drinking. Mohammed summoned him
and asked what was going on. The man replied that he had taken on a
task that was too difficult for him to do. Mohammed said that it was a
duty he should try to perform. The assassin said, "O Apostle of Allah, I
will have to tell a lie." The prophet said, "Say what you like; you are free
in the matter."

1551 The stage was set. The assassin arranged to go with a friend to the
Jew, Al Ashraf, and befriend him and discuss poetry. After friendly talk
and a few recitations, he told Al Ashraf of his dissatisfaction with Islam.
This talk bonded him to the Jew as a friend. Then he said that he wished to
borrow money to buy food and wanted to put up weapons as a security for
the loan. Also, he had some friends who were dissatisfied with Mohammed who would come as well, to get a loan and use weapons as a security.

The goal was for a small group of men to be able to approach the Jew with weapons and not arouse suspicion.

I552 The scene was set and the group of assassins met with Mohammed, and he led them to the fortified home that Al Ashraf lived in. Just before they got there, Mohammed left them with the blessing, "Go in Allah's name. O Allah, help them."

I552 They knocked on Al Ashraf's door and called out his name. He had already gone to bed when he heard them. His wife asked who was calling at that time of night. Al Ashraf told her the Muslim's name. She asked that he not go because there was bad blood between the Jews and Mohammed, and it was dangerous. He assured her that these men were no problem and went downstairs. There were the assassins with their weapons for the security of the loan and big friendly smiles. They stood outside the door and chatted. It was a beautiful night, and they invited Al Ashraf to take a short walk with them. He accepted.

I552 As they walked and talked, the lead assassin put his arm around Al Ashraf and, as he drew his arm back, ran his hand through Al Ashraf's hair. He smelled his hand and remarked upon the beautiful scent in the Jew's hair. In order to smell it better he reached up to the Jew's hair again and grabbed the hair and jerked Al Ashraf's head down. "Kill the enemy of Allah," he shouted. The assassins hacked at the Jew with their swords but in the confusion only cut him and one of their own. Then the lead assassin reached for his knife, plunged it into the Jew's belly, and ripped downwards to his groin. Al Ashraf screamed so loudly everyone woke up. The assassins ran back to Mohammed.

I552 Their wounded friend lagged behind, so they carried him back with them. When they got back to Mohammed, he was praying. They told him they had killed the enemy of Allah and their attack had terrorized all the Jews. There was no Jew in Medina who was not afraid.

> B5,59,369 *Allah's Apostle said, "Who is willing to kill Kab Bin Al-Ashraf who has hurt Allah and His Apostle?"*
>
> *Thereupon Maslama got up saying, "O Allah's Apostle! Would you like that I kill him?"*
>
> *The Prophet said, "Yes."*
>
> *Maslama said, "Then allow me to say a false thing to deceive Kab."*
>
> *The Prophet said, "You may say it."*
>
> *Then Maslama went to Kab and said, "Mohammed demands money from us and I need to borrow money."*
>
> *On that, Kab said, "By Allah, you will get tired of him!"*

Maslama said, "Now as we have followed him, we do not want to leave him unless and until we see how his end is going to be. Now we want you to lend us a camel load of food."

Kab said, "Yes, I will lend you the food, but you should mortgage something to me."

Maslama and his companion said, "What do you want?"

Kab replied, "Mortgage your women to me."

They said, "How can we mortgage our women to you and you are the most handsome of the Arabs?"

Kab said, "Then mortgage your sons to me."

They said, "How can we mortgage our sons to you? Later they would be abused by the people's saying that so-and-so has been mortgaged for a camel's load of food. That would cause us great disgrace, but we will mortgage our arms to you."

Maslama and his companion promised Kab that Maslama would return to him. He came to Kab at night along with Kab's foster brother, Abu Na'ila. Kab invited them to come into his fort, and then he went down to them.

His wife asked him, "Where are you going at this time?"

Kab replied, "None but Maslama and my foster brother Abu Na'ila has come."

His wife said, "I hear a voice as if dropping blood is from him."

Kab said, "A generous man should respond to a call at night even if invited to be killed." Maslama went with the two men.

So Maslama went in together with two men and said to them, "When Kab comes, I will touch his hair and smell it and, when you see that I have got hold of his head, strip him. I will let you smell his head."

Kab Bin Al-Ashraf came down to them wrapped in his clothes and smelling of perfume. Maslama said, "I have never smelt a better scent than this."

Kab replied, "I have the best."

Maslama requested Kab, "Will you allow me to smell your head?"

Kab said, "Yes."

Maslama smelt it and made his companion smell it as well. Then he requested Kab again, "Will you let me smell your head?" Kab said, "Yes."

When Maslama got a strong hold of him, he said to his companion, "Get at him!"

So they killed him and went to the Prophet and informed him. Abu Rafi was killed after Kab Bin Al-Ashraf.

KILL ANY JEW THAT FALLS INTO YOUR POWER

I554 The Apostle of Allah said, "Kill any Jew who falls into your power." Hearing this, Muhayyisa fell upon a Jewish merchant who was a business associate and killed him. Muhayyisa's brother was not a Muslim and asked how Muhayyisa could kill a man who had been his friend and partner in many business deals. The Muslim said that if Mohammed had asked him to kill his brother he would have done it immediately. His brother said, "You mean that if Mohammed said to cut off my head you would do it?" "Yes," was the reply. The older brother then said, "By Allah, any religion that brings you to this is marvelous." And he decided then and there to become a Muslim.

A NEW WIFE

M250 Mohammed took a third wife, Hafsa, the daughter of Omar. She was a widow of a Muslim and about 20 years old. Now he was married to daughters of two of his most faithful followers, Abu Bakr and Omar.

None of the marriages of Medina would ever produce children who lived to be adults. Only his first marriage in Mecca produced a child who would give him grandchildren who lived to adulthood. Fatima, his daughter, would continue the lineage of Mohammed.

A SETBACK

CHAPTER 15

*8:13 This was because they opposed Allah and
His messenger. Ones who oppose Allah and His
messenger will be severely punished by Allah.*

THE BATTLE OF UHUD

1555 Back at Mecca those who had lost at the Battle of Badr told others, "Men of Quraysh, Mohammed has killed your best men. Give us money so we may take revenge." Money was raised, men were hired, and an army was put together.

1557 One of the Quraysh had a black slave who could throw a spear and never miss the mark. He made a deal with the slave: "If you kill Hamza, then I will free you." Hamza had killed the Quraysh's uncle at Badr and was Mohammed's uncle.

1558 So the Meccans camped near Medina, ready for war, ready for revenge. The Muslims now needed a strategy. Many, including Mohammed, wanted to sit and let the Meccans attack them. The town itself could be used in a defensive way—walls and rooftops would give any defender a strong advantage. But blood ran hot in the Muslim warriors. They were not afraid to meet the Meccans on the field of combat man to man. After Badr, they were invincible; Allah had said as much. "Mohammed, lead us to our enemies," they said. "Don't let them think we are weak cowards." The arguments continued until Mohammed went in his house and came out in his armor.

1559 But now, seeing him in his armor, the hot-bloods repented and said they should never have tried to persuade Mohammed. They admitted they had been wrong. Mohammed said, "When a prophet puts on his armor, he should not take it off until there has been war." So he marched out with a thousand men to meet the Meccans. But the uncertainties continued; one of the clan leaders of three hundred men said there was no reason to be there and turned his men toward home. Mohammed cursed them and kept on going toward the battlefield.

1560 When he saw the Meccans, Mohammed said, "Let there be no fighting until I give the word." What he saw made his blood boil. The Meccans had turned their camels and horses loose in the crops of the Medinans. Mohammed placed fifty archers to protect his rear and flank and told them to hold their ground. Mohammed put on a second coat of armor.

I561 Mohammed took his sword, thrust it into the air, and cried, "Who will take this sword with its right (use it as it should be used)?" Two different men stood to take it, and he turned away from them. One man asked what was the right. Mohammed said, "That you should strike the enemy until it breaks or bends." The man took the sword. He put a red turban on his head and strutted in front of the Muslims, waving the sword at the Meccans.

> M31,6040 *Anas reported that Allah's Messenger took hold of his sword on the Day of Uhud and said, "Who would take it from me?"*
>
> *All the persons stretched their hands saying, "I would do it, I would do it."*
>
> *Allah's Apostle said, "Who would take it in order to fulfil its rights (use it as it should be used) ?"*
>
> *Then the people withdrew their hands. Abu Dujana said, "I am here to take it and fulfil its rights." He took it and struck the heads of the polytheists.*

> M31,5932 *During the Battle of Uhud a polytheist fiercely attacked the Muslims. Mohammed said, "Sad, shoot an arrow."*
>
> *Sad said, "May my mother and father be taken as ransom for you." He drew an arrow and shot a featherless arrow at the polytheist aiming at his side. He fell down and his private parts were exposed. Allah's Messenger laughed so that I saw his front teeth.*

I562 Abu Sufyan, the chief of the Meccans, spoke to his standard-bearers. "You had charge of our flag at Badr and you saw what happened. The fortunes of an army depend upon the standard. You must guard it well or you need to give it to us and we will save you the trouble." The standard-bearer was incensed. "You want us to surrender the banner to you? Just wait until tomorrow and see what we do!" Abu Sufyan was pleased and smiled inside.

I562 The morrow came and the battle began. The Meccans had brought their women for the sole purpose of urging the men on. Men do not want to be cowards in front of women. The women began to beat their tambourines and chant poetry:

> *If you advance we will hug you*
> *And place soft rugs beneath you.*

If you retreat we will leave you,
Leave and no more love you.

I564 Hamza fought like a lion. He was big and skilled and killed many Meccans. As he approached one, he cried, "Come here, you son of a clitoris cutter!" (The Meccan warrior's mother performed the operation of removing the clitoris from young girls.) Hamza struck and killed the man in a blow. Lurking around the edges of the battle was the black slave charged with killing Hamza. He had watched and waited, and now he stepped forth and threw his spear like an athlete. He never missed, and he did not miss now. The spear stuck Hamza in the belly and exited. Hamza strode toward the slave but staggered and fell. The slave watched and waited as Hamza slowly died. When he was dead, the now freed slave stepped up, withdrew his spear, and walked off the field. He had done his job, and he left a free man.

I566 The freed slave lived in Mecca until Mohammed captured the town. He was afraid of Mohammed until someone suggested he convert so Mohammed would forgive him. When Mohammed heard that the man who had killed his uncle had submitted to Islam, he remarked, "Leave him alone. The submission of one man is better than the killing of a thousand unbelievers."

I570 The Muslims fought without any fear and the battle went against the Meccans, who were cut off from their camp. The camp had the treasure—the spoils of war—and the Muslim archers left their positions to get to the spoils. The battle might go to Islam, but the archers would have the treasure. This left the army's flank and rear open and the Meccan cavalry took advantage and charged the rear. Mohammed was in the rear. The battle suddenly went against Islam.

I571 The Muslims were put to flight and many were slain. Even Mohammed got hit in the face by a rock, broke a tooth, and split his lip. He was incensed. The Meccans were all around and the Muslims had to protect him with their bodies.

> M19,4413 *When the enemy got the upper hand on the day of the Battle of Uhud, Mohammed was left with only seven men from the Helpers and two men from the Quraysh [the Immigrants]. When the enemy advanced toward him and overwhelmed him, he said, "Who so turns them away from us will attain Paradise or will be my Companion in Paradise."*
>
> *A man from the Helpers came forward and fought the enemy until he was killed. The enemy advanced and overwhelmed him again, and Mohammed repeated the words, "Who turns them*

away from us will attain Paradise or will be my Companion in Paradise." A man from the Helpers came forward and fought until he was killed. This state continued until the seven Helpers were killed one after the other.

Now Mohammed said to his two Companions, "We have not done justice to our Companions."

M19,4414 *On the day of the Battle of Uhud the face of Mohammed was injured, his front teeth were damaged, and his helmet was crushed. Fatima, the daughter of Mohammed, was washing the blood from his head, and Ali was pouring water on it from a shield. When Fatima saw that the bleeding had increased on account of pouring water on the wound, she took a piece of mat and burnt it until it was reduced to ashes. She put the ashes on the wound and the bleeding stopped.*

I574 At one point the Meccans thought they had killed the man who had brought them so much pain. One Muslim recognized the prophet under his helmet and spread the news that he was alive. Mohammed fled the field. He was a heavy man and, in addition, wearing two suits of armor. He almost could not climb the rocks and hill without help.

I583 The day went to the Meccans, the Quraysh. They did not press their advantage. They had come to extract tribal justice, and they killed about as many of the Muslims as they had lost at Badr. Abu Sufyan, the Meccan leader, agreed through an emissary that they would meet in combat the following year.

I581 After the battle was over, some of the Meccan women who had been "cheerleaders" for their troops went onto the battlefield and cut off the noses and ears of the Muslim dead and made jewelry of the pieces. From Hamza, Mohammed's favorite warrior, they even removed the liver. One of the women wrote this poem:

We have paid you back for Badr
And a war that follows a war is violent.
I could not bear the loss of my friends
Nor my brother and his uncle and my first born.
I have slaked my vengeance and fulfilled my vow.
The slave who killed Hamza has cooled the burning in my breast.
I shall thank the slave, now free,
Until my bones rot in the grave. —Hind d. Utba

I584 After Badr, the Meccans had mourned their nobility and heroes. Now it was Mohammed's turn to mourn. The Koran changed every Muslim corpse into a martyr in the pleasure gardens of heaven.

1586 The dead Muslims were buried in the battlefield. Mohammed said, "I testify that those who are wounded in jihad will be raised by Allah, with his bleeding wounds smelling like the finest perfume." When Mohammed heard the women weeping for their dead, he wanted wailing for his Uncle Hamza as well. So the women wailed for Hamza and Mohammed felt better.

1587 When Mohammed entered his house he handed his sword to his daughter and told her, "Wash the blood from this for, by Allah, it has served me well today." The next day he ordered all the fighters who had been at Uhud to marshal themselves and be ready to head out to pursue the enemy. This move was pure strategy to impress upon the enemy that he was still strong and not weakened by his losses. They went about eight miles from Medina and camped for three days before returning to Medina.

1589 Mohammed was the supreme master of the psychology of war. He sent an agent to Abu Sufyan who pretended to be a friend of the Meccans. Abu Sufyan was thinking about going back and finishing off the Muslims. But Mohammed's agent told Abu Sufyan that Mohammed was coming very soon with an army, the like of which had never been seen. The Muslims were in a state of total fury and would sweep into Hell all who were in front of them. Abu Sufyan, a merchant, left for Mecca and security. The Meccans had settled their tribal score.

THE KORAN AND THE BATTLE OF UHUD

Since Allah had sent angels to the previous Battle of Badr and the outnumbered Muslims triumphed, how could they fail at Uhud? The Koran spends some sixty verses explaining how this happened and how the results were further proof of the alliance between Allah and Mohammed.

1593 Two of the Muslim clans had had doubts about the battle. But Allah was their God, and they did not doubt Islam and went on into the battle because of their belief in Allah and Mohammed.

> 3:121 *Remember when you [Mohammed] left your home early in the morning to lead the believers to their battle stations? Allah heard and knew all. When two of your brigades showed cowardice, Allah protected them both.*

1595 The reason for the Muslim loss was that the archers did not hold their ground. When they saw that the Meccans were cut off from their camp, they ran to get the treasure of war. Greed caused them to disobey Mohammed. They were told they should always obey Mohammed; he spoke for the Lord of all.

3:131 *Obey Allah and His messenger so that you may receive mercy.*

1595 Those who did not follow orders should ask for forgiveness. If they realized the loss was their fault and were remorseful, they would still get their reward of heaven.

3:133 *Urge each other on to earn forgiveness from your Lord, and the Paradise as wide as heaven and earth is prepared for the righteous. Those who give freely, whether they are prosperous or poor; who control their anger; who are forgiving (for Allah loves those who do good); who, when they have sinned or wronged themselves, go to Allah and implore His forgiveness for their sins (for who except Allah can forgive you of your sins?) and do not knowingly continue in their sinning; these will be rewarded with their Lord's forgiveness and with the Garden watered by flowing rivers where they will live forever.*

1597 The reason Allah let the Meccans win was to test the Muslims. Now they truly knew themselves. Were they fair-weather friends of Mohammed, or could they see their faults? If they obeyed Mohammed, then they could become true Muslims. A true Muslim never lost his morale, never fell into despair.

3:139 *Therefore, do not lose heart or despair; if you are a true believer, you will be victorious.*

1596 There were casualties, and they had suffered losses in the battle, but they had to remember the non-Muslims had also suffered. Over the long view, fortunes went up and down. They had to take the long view and believe in Mohammed and know that all would turn out well in the end. Those who died had the best reward. They were martyrs for Islam. Those really in the wrong were the hypocrites, the pretenders.

3:140 *If you have been wounded, be certain that the same has already befallen your enemies. We bring misfortune to mankind in turns so that Allah can discern who are the true believers and so that We may select martyrs from among you. Allah does not love those who do evil.*

1596 The Muslims had to realize that Allah would purify them through tests such as the one at Uhud. Those of true faith would not be discouraged, but the hypocrites would be exposed and deprived of all blessing.

3:141 *It is also Allah's purpose to test the believers and to destroy the unbelievers.*

1596 Did they think they would get to heaven before Allah had tested them? Allah surely knew who was really a believer. A Muslim warrior had to be given a trial, and losing at Uhud was merely a trial.

> 3:142 *Did you think that you would be permitted into Paradise before Allah tested you to see who would fight for His cause [jihad] and endure until the end?*

1596 Those who had not taken part in the big victory at Badr were anxious to show off as warriors, but when the actual killing started many were not as good as they thought they would be.

> 3:143 *You used to wish for death before you saw it, but now that you have seen it with your own eyes, you turn and run from it.*

1597 The Muslims should not think they were the first to experience failure. In history many had failed in jihad, but they never lost heart or weakened. The lesson of Uhud was to be firm and not get depressed over a small failure.

> 3:146 *Many of the messengers have fought for Allah's cause [jihad] alongside large armies. They were never frightened by what they encountered on Allah's path, nor did they weaken or cringe with fear. Allah loves those who stand firm.*

1599 Jihad wasn't over. Soon Islam would bring terror to the unbelievers. After death they would burn in Hell. Their destruction would come because they did not believe in the religion of Islam.

> 3:151 *We will strike terror into the hearts of the unbelievers because they worship others besides Allah, which He gave them no permission to do. Their home will be the Fire, a terrible resting place for the evil-doers.*

1599 The slaughter of unbelievers at Badr had gone well and they were about to wipe the unbelievers off the face of the earth, thanks to Allah. But then they disobeyed Mohammed. Allah did not destroy them because he was merciful, but their greed for the treasure (spoils of war) was of this world. They had to desire what comes after death, not the wealth of this world. They had to learn this lesson with the grace of Allah.

> 3:152 *Allah fulfilled His covenant with you [Mohammed] when He allowed you to destroy your enemies. And then later, when you [the Muslims at Uhud] lost your courage, arguments broke out among you and you sinned after you had come so close to what you wanted. Some of you wish for the desires of this world and some of you for the world to come. Therefore, He caused you to be defeated so that you might be tested. Now He has forgiven you for Allah shows grace to the believers.*

1601 Some accepted the loss but others were anxious because they did not trust Allah. The hypocrites divorced themselves from the decision and blamed others for the failure. If they had had their way, then everyone would have been safe. But when Allah decreed one's time had come, nothing could stay the hand of death. Death would come, and it was better to die in jihad.

> 3:154 *Then, after the trouble Allah sent down upon you, He sent down calmness to wash over some of you. Some were overtaken by sleep, and others lay awake, stirred by their own passions, ignorantly thinking unjust thoughts about Allah. And they ask, "What do we gain by this affair?" Say: Truly the affair is entirely in Allah's hands. They hide in their hearts that which they do not want to tell you. They speak out saying, "If we had any say in this affair then none of us would have been killed here." Say: If you had stayed at home, those of you who were destined to be killed would have died regardless. This has taken place so that Allah might test your faith and see what is in your hearts. Allah knows the deepest secrets of every heart.*

1602 Mohammed would be gentle with the Muslims, overlook their faults, and forgive them. He would still consult them from time to time, but all final decisions lay with Allah and Mohammed.

> 3:158 *It was because of Allah's mercy that you spoke so gently to them. For if you had dealt with them severely or been hard-hearted, they would have turned away from you. Therefore, forgive them and ask Allah to forgive them and counsel them in the affair of war; and when you have resolved the matters, put your trust in Allah. Allah loves those who trust Him. If Allah is helping you, no one can defeat you. But if He leaves you, who will be there to help you when He is gone? Therefore, let the faithful put their trust in Allah.*

1603 The Muslims' loss was a test brought on by their decisions. The hypocrites were told to fight in jihad or at least defend the city. Their excuses were those of an unbeliever.

> 3:166 *The destruction which befell you the day the two armies met in battle was Allah's will so He would recognize who were the true believers and who were the hypocrites. And when they were told, "Come and fight for Allah's cause [jihad] and drive your enemies back," they replied, "If we knew how to fight, then we would have followed you."*
> 3:168 *Some of them were closer to unbelief than faith that day. What they said with their mouths was not what was in their hearts, but Allah knew what they were hiding in their hearts. It was these who said, while sitting at home, of their brothers, "If only they had listened to us, then they*

would not have been killed." Say: Try to avert your death if what you say is true!

1606 The success the unbelievers were experiencing was temporary. They would grow in their evil and be punished.

3:178 *Do not let the unbelievers think that we lengthen their days for their own good. We give them time only hoping that they will commit more serious sins. They will receive a shameful punishment.*

POETRY FROM THE MUSLIMS

We attacked you with Allah's help and sustenance.
Our spearheads directed toward you.
Our lances made gaping wounds among you
Like the mouths of water-skins where the water gushes forth.
We thrust our swords between your shoulders
Where they drank blood again and again.
We made your shit run thin out your asses
Like a camel with diarrhea.
We, and not men like you—children of your mother's ass,
Meet the fighters when adversity comes.

THE BETRAYAL

1638 One of the tribes south of Medina sent an envoy to Mohammed and asked that he send men who could instruct the tribe in Islam. So Mohammed happily sent six men. When they got near the town where the tribe lived they stopped to rest.

1639 While they were resting, they were surprised to see men with drawn swords approaching. They grabbed their own swords and faced the approaching men. The men told the Muslims they had no intention of harming them but wanted to take them to Mecca and deliver them there. They would be paid, and then the Meccans would ransom them to Mohammed for a profit and vengeance. The Muslims relaxed once their lives were not in danger.

1639 One of the Muslims said he would never trust a non-Muslim and that he was a warrior and would die then and there. So they fought, and three of the Muslims were killed. The remaining three wanted to save their lives and surrendered.

1640 They were bound and taken to Mecca. On the way, one of them loosed himself and grabbed a sword. The gang drew back and threw stones until they killed him. In Mecca the other two were sold. The buyers took them outside the sacred area of Mecca. Both of the buyers had vengeance in mind when they bought the men. One of the buyers crucified his purchased Muslim. As he died he cursed each one of them that they might die one by one.

ASSASSINATION AS JIHAD

M276 After Uhud, several tribes allied themselves under the leadership of Sufyan Ibn Khalid. Mohammed dispatched an assassin to kill him, for without his leadership the coalition would fall apart. The assassin, Abdullah, joined Sufyan's forces and waited until he was alone with him. He killed him and cut off his head and went back to Medina.

M276 When Abdullah got back, he went straight to the mosque where he knew Mohammed always was. Mohammed welcomed him and asked for a report. Abdullah presented Mohammed the head of his enemy. Mohammed was gratified and presented him his walking stick. He said, "This is a token between you and me on the day of resurrection. Very few will have such to lean on in that day." Abdullah attached it to his sword scabbard.

TREACHERY AND A LETHAL MISTAKE

T1442 Another tribe sent an envoy to Mohammed to ask him to come teach Islam. He offered Mohammed a present, but Mohammed would not take a gift from a non-Muslim. He then preached Islam to the envoy; however, Mohammed was reluctant to send anyone to preach Islam, due to the previous ambush of his men.

I649 Discussions were held and Mohammed felt comfortable with sending seventy of his fighters. When the seventy fighters got to the tribe, they got off their camels and sent two men to pasture them. Very soon they found themselves surrounded by men on horses wielding swords with blood in their eyes. The Muslims fought to the last man, who actually was found wounded but alive and lived to die at the Battle of the Trench.

I650 The two Muslims with the pastured camels noticed buzzards circling and rushed to find their men. The killers were still there on horseback. One of the Muslims said they should run and tell Mohammed. The other man said he could not leave his dearest friend's body and pulled his sword. He was quickly cut down. The other Muslim surrendered.

I650 The enemy cut off the Muslim's forelock (a humiliation for an Arab) and set him free due to complicated tribal relations between him and the killers' tribe. He rode off, and later, on the trail back to Medina, he fell in with two Arabs of a tribe related to the ones who had killed his friends. They sat and talked, and then the two men napped. The Muslim killed both of them. There was a problem, however, in that the clan they belonged to had a special treaty with Mohammed.

1650 The fighter went back to Medina and gave a full report to Mohammed. It was a very bad day for Mohammed. Sixty-nine of his best men killed, and now he owed blood money for the killing of two men of a clan with which he had an alliance.

THE JEWS AGAIN

CHAPTER 16

*8.46 Obey Allah and His messenger, and do not argue
with one another for fear that you will lose courage and
strength. Be patient for Allah is with the patient.*

CLEANSING

1652 It was four years since Mohammed had come to Medina. He went
to one of the two remaining Jewish tribes, the Bin Al-Nadir, seeking a loan
to pay the blood money for the two men his fighter had killed. At first they
agreed, but as they talked about it more they decided it would be a good
time to kill Mohammed. There he was in their quarter, sitting on a wall
near a roof. Why not send a man up to drop a rock on the man who had
been such a sorrow to them? Mohammed got wind of the plan and left.

1653 This was as good a reason as any to deal with the Jews—the same
Jews who insisted he was not the prophet. He raised his army and went off
to put the Jews under siege. The Jews lived in a fortified area where they
were farmers and grew the finest dates in all of Arabia. Mohammed cut
and burned their date palms as they watched. They called out, "You have
prohibited wanton destruction and blamed those who do that. Now you
do what you forbid."

1653 The other Jewish tribe had assured their brothers they would come
to their defense, but no one did. So, with no help from their brothers, the
besieged Jews cut a deal with the Apostle of Allah. If he spared their lives
they would leave, taking what they could carry on their camels, except
their armor.

1653 They loaded their camels and even tore down their homes to get
the wood to take with them. Wood was precious in Arabia. And so the Jews
left the town of Medina. Some went to Syria and others went to Khaybar.
They would live to regret that destination.

1654 When there was fighting in jihad, the fighters got four fifths of the
spoils of war. But since there had been no fighting, there was no reason to
give four fifths to the jihadists. All of the spoils of war went to Mohammed, not just one fifth.

1654 The incident created some new theological problems for Mohammed—the burning of the date palms and his getting all the money. The

Koran had all the answers. It was Allah who had wreaked his vengeance upon the Jews and given Mohammed power over them. It was even Allah who caused the Jews to tear down their own houses.

59:2 *It was He who caused the People of the Book [the Jews] to leave their homes and go into the first exile. They did not think they would leave, and they thought that their fortresses could protect them from Allah. But Allah's wrath reached them from where they did not expect it and cast terror into their hearts, so that they destroyed their homes with their own hands, as well as by the hands of the believers. Take warning from this example, you who have the eyes to see it!*

B4,52,153 *Because the property of the Jews that Allah had given to Mohammed had not been won by the Muslims through the use of their horses and camels, it belonged exclusively to Mohammed. He used it to give his family their yearly allowance and he spent the rest on weapons and horses for jihad.*

I654 The Jews were very fortunate that Allah let them go with a few worldly processions. They got out alive and Allah did not slay them, but they would burn in Hell since they resisted Mohammed.

59:3 *And if Allah had not decreed their exile, surely He would have punished them in this world. And in the world to come they will receive the punishment of the Fire because they had disobeyed Allah and His Messenger. Whoever disobeys Allah, knows that Allah is truly severe in His punishment.*

I654 As for the wanton destruction of the palm trees, it was nothing one way or the other. And it was certainly no fault of Mohammed's; it was the Jews' fault. They should have done what Allah wanted, and then they would not have suffered Allah's vengeance.

59:5 *Allah gave you permission to cut down some palm trees and leave others intact so as to shame the wicked [the Jews].*

I654 As for all the spoils of war going to Mohammed, there had been no actual fighting, hence there was no need to give spoils to fighters. Mohammed could do as he wished.

59:7 *The spoils of war taken from the people in the cities and given by Allah to His Messenger belong to Allah, to His Messenger and to his family, to the orphans, to the poor, and to the wayfaring traveler so that it will not stay among those of you who are wealthy. Take what the Messenger has offered you, and refuse what he has forbidden you. And fear Allah, for Allah is severe in His punishment.*

THE BATTLE OF THE DITCH

CHAPTER 17

24:31 But when Allah and His Messenger call the true
believers to judge between them, their response is, "We
have heard, and we obey." These are the ones who will
be successful. Those who obey Allah and His Messenger
and who dread and fear Allah will be the winners.

THE NEXT RAID

I662 After the second of the three clans of Jews had been cleansed from
Medina there was no violence for nearly two months. Then Mohammed
led his men out to fight an Arab tribe, a large group of non-believers who
were well armed. No fighting occurred as each was afraid of the other.

THE LAST EXPEDITION TO BADR

I666 Mohammed had been in Medina four years. It had been a year
since the Battle of Badr, and it was time to meet the Meccans as promised.
He went to Badr and waited for eight days. Abu Sufyan set out with his
army to Badr, but it had been a dry year and there was no pasture for the
animals; and no pasture meant no milk from the animals for food. Abu
Sufyan decided to turn back and wait another year and hope for enough
rain for good pasture. The only damage to the Meccans was some insult-
ing poetry written by Muslims.

WIVES FOUR AND FIVE

M289 It had been about a year since his last marriage and now Mohammed added a new wife, Zaynab, who was the widow of his cousin killed at
Badr. She only lived a year or two and was noted for her charity. His next
wife, Um Salaam, was a widow as well; her husband had been critically
wounded at Uhud.

MARRIAGE TO HIS DAUGHTER-IN-LAW

M290 Mohammed had an adopted son, Zayd, and one day he went by
his house. Mohammed went inside but Zayd was not there. The next part

is not clear, but Mohammed saw his daughter-in-law, Zaynab, in a thin dress, and her charms were evident. Mohammed was smitten and said, "Gracious Lord! Good Heavens! How you turn the hearts of men!"

M290 Zaynab had indeed turned the head of the future king of Arabia, and she told her husband what Mohammed had said. The stepson went to Mohammed and said he would divorce Zaynab so he could have her. Mohammed said no, but Zayd went ahead and divorced her anyway. In Arabia, a union between a man and his daughter-in-law was incest and forbidden. While Mohammed was with Aisha he had a revelation and said, "Who will go and congratulate Zaynab and tell her that Allah has blessed our marriage?" The maid went right off to tell her the good news. So Mohammed added another wife—his ex–daughter-in-law. Since Zayd was not really a son, there was no incest.

M291 Aisha never liked the beautiful Zaynab. Since the permission to marry had come from Allah, Zaynab lorded it over the other wives. They had been chosen by Mohammed, but she had been chosen by Allah. The Koran:

> 33:4 *Allah has not given any man two hearts for one body, nor has He made your wives whom you divorce to be like your mothers, nor has He made your adopted sons like your real sons. [Previous to this verse, an Arab's adopted children were treated as blood children. This verse relates to verse 37 of this sura.] These are only words you speak with your mouths, but Allah speaks the truth and guides to the right path. Name your adopted sons after their real fathers; this is more just in Allah's sight. But if you do not know their fathers' names, call them your brothers in the faith and your friends. There will be no blame on you if you sin unintentionally, but that which you intend in your heart will be held against you. Allah is forgiving and merciful.*

> 33:37 *And remember when you said to your adopted son [Zayd], the one who had received Allah's favor [converted to Islam], "Keep your wife to yourself and fear Allah," and you hid in your heart what Allah was to reveal, and you feared men [what people would say if he married his daughter-in-law], when it would have been right that you should fear Allah. And when Zayd divorced his wife, We gave her to you as your wife, so it would not be a sin for believers to marry the wives of their adopted sons, after they have divorced them. And Allah's will must be carried out.*

M292 It was about this time that the veil was imposed on women. No longer would any man, except the wife's relatives, see the face of any of Mohammed's wives. Mohammed now had many wives, and people were in and out of his apartments. He had just seen what happened when men saw young and beautiful women. His wives became "mothers of the faithful" and could not marry after Mohammed died.

THE RAID ON DUMATUL JANDAL

1668 Mohammed returned to Medina and rested for some months. Then he set out on a raid to Dumatul Jandal but found no success in locating the enemy nonbelievers.

THE BATTLE OF THE DITCH

1669 Some of the Jews decided they needed to destroy Mohammed, and to do that they needed allies. Since allies were to be found in Mecca, they went there and parleyed with the leaders of the Quraysh. Since this was a war of religion, the first thing the Quraysh wanted was proof of religious supremacy to Mohammed. The leaders said to the Jews, "You are people of the book, and you know our disagreement. Who has the better religion, the Quraysh or Mohammed?" The leaders of the Jews replied that the Quraysh had the better religion.

1669 So the Koran says:

> 4:51 *Have you not seen those [Jews allied with the Meccans] to whom part of the Scriptures were given? They believe in idols and sorcery, and they say of the unbelievers, "These are guided on a better path than the believers." It is on these whom Allah has laid His curse. Those who are cursed by Allah will have no one to help them.*

1669 That answer put the Quraysh in a good mood, and they were willing to fight Mohammed. Then the same Jews went to the Arab tribe of the Ghatafans and made an alliance with them to fight Mohammed.

1670 Mohammed had many spies in Mecca, so in no time he knew of the coming fight, and he set out to prepare for it. A Persian suggested to Mohammed that he build a trench as a barrier against the Meccans and their allies. Although this type of warfare was unknown to the Arabs, Mohammed was the supreme master of war and saw that it would give a good defense. For eight days the Arabs worked at building a trench around the weak points of Medina. To help with morale, Mohammed personally pitched in and took his turn at manual labor.

1671 Not predisposed to hard manual labor, the trench-diggers often left work early. The labor problems even worked their way into the Koran:

> 24:62 *Only those who believe in Allah and His Messenger are the true believers, and when they are gathered together, do not leave until they have sought his permission. Those who ask your permission are the ones*

who truly believe in Allah and His Messenger. And when they ask your permission to leave for personal reasons, give permission to whom you please, and ask Allah for His indulgence on their behalf, for Allah is indulgent, merciful.

I673 The work was done just in time. The Quraysh and the other allies camped near the trench. Mohammed and his army camped on their side of the trench and sent the women and children to the forts.

I674 A Jew who had been exiled from Medina and moved to Mecca went to the last remaining Jewish tribe in Medina. The Jewish forts were outside the city and the trench defending Medina. At first the Jewish chief would not even open the door to the Jewish ally of the Meccans, but he relented when the visitor said the chief would not admit him because he was too stingy to feed him. At the insult to his hospitality, the Jewish chief opened the fort door. Once inside the visitor said, "Kab, I have brought you a great army and a chance for immortal fame. I am here with the Quraysh and their allies who want to crush our common enemy, Mohammed. We will not leave until we destroy him." The chief replied, "You are a rain cloud with thunder and lightning but no rain. Go away." And they argued back and forth. The visitor said that, if the allies left without killing Mohammed, then he would come back to the fort and await a common fortune with the last clan of Jews in Medina.

I675 The Jewish chief relented and agreed to help. Mohammed's spies brought him this news before nightfall. So Mohammed sent his own agents to speak with the chief of the Jews. If the discussion went well, they could announce it to all; but, if not, they were to use coded language so they would not lessen the Muslims' morale.

I675 The agents returned with a coded message: The last of the Jewish tribes was not going to help Mohammed. Coding the message had not helped morale; as time dragged on, muttering started inside the Muslim camp. One man said they had been promised the wealth of Rome and Persia and they were not even able to go to the privy safely. Another clan chief talked in public about leaving and going to his home.

I676 Time pressed on for twenty days, and the Meccans were not capable of dealing with a new defensive strategy, the trench. They weren't helped by the custom of rotating the overall command on a daily basis to different chiefs.

I677 Mohammed was in a bad spot, but his morale never flagged. His creativity in war showed itself again. He had said that war was deception and now was the time to put it to use. He sent an agent to the largest of the allies of the Quraysh, the Ghatafans. Mohammed proposed a deal. The

Ghatafans would go back home and Mohammed would pay them a third of the date crop of Medina the following year. There was a tentative agreement. When Mohammed talked about the plan with the two Medinan Arab clan chiefs, they balked. Basically, they said the Ghatafans could go to Hell; they would never impoverish themselves for nonbelievers. Mohammed went along with them.

1677 The "war" dragged on. A small party of the Meccans crossed the trench and skirmished, losing one man. Arrows were shot across the trench without effect. One arrow did hit Sad, chief of a Medinan clan. The small wound in his arm would play a great role later, but it was of no tactical importance now.

1681 One of the Ghatafans approached Mohammed saying he was a Muslim but no one else knew it. Mohammed told him, "Go and sow distrust among our enemies. War is deceit."

B4,52,268 *Mohammed said, "War is deceit."*

1681 Off the secret agent went to the Jews of Medina, for he had been a great "friend" of theirs in the past. Talking to the chief, the agent reminded him of the good times and then argued that, when the war was over, the Jews of Medina would still be in Medina and the Quraysh, the Ghatafans, and the rest of the Meccans and their allies would go home. And where would that leave the Jews? If things went badly the others could cut and run, but the Jews could not. He advised them not to fight alongside the Meccans. After the Meccans were gone, the Jews would be subject to Mohammed's vengeance. "Before you fight alongside them," Mohammed's agent said, "demand that the Meccans send you some of their sons as hostages to ensure that they will fight and won't leave you alone to suffer."

"Good advice," thought the Jews.

1681 The agent then went to Abu Sufyan and told him of his affection for him and his tribe. He had some confidential information that Abu Sufyan needed to know. Could he keep this quiet? He told them, "The Jews have regretted siding with you against Mohammed. They have a deal with him. They plan to ask for some of your chiefs and sons so they can be handed over to Mohammed. If the Jews ask for security hostages, don't do it."

1682 Next the agent of Mohammed went to the Ghatafan Arabs. He told them he was their best friend and repeated what he had told the Quraysh.

1682 Time was running out. The weather was bad. Food for troops and fodder for the animals was in short supply. It was time to finish this war. The Meccans and the Ghatafans sent representatives to the Jews of Medina and said it was time to fight and they needed to fulfill their end of the deal and send warriors. The Jews told them the next day was the Sabbath and they would not fight on their holy day. They would need some security hostages to ensure that the Meccans and their allies did not run off and leave the Jews to Mohammed alone.

I682 When the representatives came back with this message, it was very clear that the Jews were traitors and that Mohammed's agent had told them the truth. They were allies no more, the lying Jews and the Meccans.

> B4,52,86 *Mohammed said, "When you face your enemy be patient."*

I683 That night was miserable—rainy, with a very cold wind. The next morning, Abu Sufyan, the chief of the Quraysh, saddled his camel and said, "This is not a permanent camp; our horses and camels are dying. I am leaving and you can do as you wish." The Meccans left as losers. Mohammed had won again.

THE ATTEMPTED ASSASSINATION OF ABU SUFYAN

T1438 Mohammed sent two men to Mecca to kill his rival, Abu Sufyan. The plan was simple and the leader was from Mecca so he knew it well. They set out on one camel for Abu Sufyan's home where one man would stand watch and the other would go in and put a knife in him. But the assisting Muslim wanted to go to the Kabah and pray. The leader argued against it because he was well known, but the other Muslim insisted. So they went to the Kabah and, sure enough, the leader was recognized. The Meccans set up a cry of alarm and the men fled Mecca. There was no way to kill Abu Sufyan now.

T1439 The Muslims ran to a cave on the outskirts of Mecca. They placed rocks in front of the cave and waited quietly. A Meccan approached the cave while cutting grass for his horse. The Muslim leader came out of the cave and killed him with a knife thrust to the belly. The man screamed loudly, and his companions came running; however, they were more concerned with their dying comrade than the killers and left carrying the body. The Muslims waited for a while and then fled again.

T1440 On their way back to Medina, the Muslims met a one-eyed shepherd. It turned out that they were related by clan ties. The shepherd said he was not a Muslim nor would he ever be. As they sat talking, the shepherd lay back and went to sleep. The leader took his bow and drove its tip down through the shepherd's one eye, into his brain, and out the back of his head. Then they headed on back to Medina.

T1440 On the road, the leader saw two Meccans who were enemies of Islam. He shot one and captured the other and marched him to Medina. When they got to Mohammed with the captive and told him the whole story of the killing, Mohammed laughed so hard they could see his back teeth. Then he blessed them.

THE LAST JEWS OF MEDINA

CHAPTER 18

*33:21 You have an excellent example in Allah's Messenger
for those of you who put your hope in Allah and the
Last Day and who praise Allah continually.*

THE LAST SOLUTION FOR THE JEWS

I684 That same day the angel Gabriel came to Mohammed at noon and asked if Mohammed were through fighting. Gabriel and the angels were going to attack the last Jewish tribe in Medina, the Bin Qurayzah. Gabriel said, "Allah commands you to go to the Jews. I am headed there now to shake their stronghold."

> B4,52,68 *During the Battle of the Trench, Mohammed paused from fighting, stripped off his weapons, and bathed. Gabriel, covered in dust, revealed himself to Mohammed and said, "You have laid down your weapons. I have not laid my arms down yet."*
> *Mohammed asked, "Where do you want me to go?"*
> *Gabriel said, "That way," pointing toward the Jewish camp.*
> *Mohammed armed himself and marched into battle.*

I684 Mohammed called upon his troops, and they headed for the Jews. Mohammed rode up to the forts and called out, "You brothers of apes, has Allah disgraced you and brought His vengeance upon you?"

I685 Mohammed put the Jews under siege for twenty-five days. The Jews, for their own reasons, had not laid in stores for a siege. They had three choices. One was to submit to Islam, but they would not abandon their religion.

I685 The second choice was to kill their women and children so they would not be hindered by sentiment and could come out of their forts and die like men. But they could not stand the thought of killing their own. The third choice was to attack.

I686 The following day was the Sabbath. Perhaps Mohammed wouldn't expect them to fight, and they could surprise with an attack. Then again, the Jews did not want to violate the Sabbath.

1686 The Jews asked Mohammed to send them a man they thought was a friend. He came as requested. They asked him if they should surrender to Mohammed's judgment. The Muslim said yes but, as soon as they did, Mohammed would—then he drew his finger across his throat. The next morning the Jews surrendered to Mohammed anyway.

1689 It was judgment day. One of the two Arab tribes in Medina had been an ally of these Jews, so a tribal chief, Sad, was selected to judge them. Now, Sad had been wounded at the Battle of the Trench and was suffering from an infected wound that was to kill him on the morrow. On this day he was to be judge and jury. He was brought from Mohammed's hospital area to make his pronouncement. It was simple. Kill all the men. Take their property and take the women and children as captives. Mohammed said, "You have given the judgment of Allah."

> B5,58,148 *When some of the remaining Jews of Medina agreed to obey a verdict from Sad, Mohammed sent for him. He approached the mosque riding a donkey and Mohammed said, "Stand up for your leader." Mohammed then said, "Sad, give these people your verdict."*
>
> *Sad replied, "Their soldiers should be beheaded, and their women and children should become slaves."*
>
> *Mohammed, pleased with the verdict, said, "You have made a ruling that Allah or a king would approve of."*

1690 The captives were taken into Medina, where they dug mass graves in the marketplace. It was a long day, but eight hundred Jews met their death that day. Mohammed and his twelve-year-old wife sat and watched the executions the entire day and into the night. The Apostle of Allah had every adult male Jew killed. For every Jewish male, pubic hair was a death sentence. If he had no pubic hair, then he would be raised as a Muslim.

1691 There was one Jewish woman killed on that day. She sat and talked with Mohammed's child-wife, Aisha. When her time came, she got up, went over to the graves in good spirits, and was killed.

1691 There was one old Jew who had saved the life of one of the Muslims. The Muslim went to Mohammed and asked for leniency for the Jew. Mohammed agreed. When the old Jew was told he was spared, he then asked for his family to be spared. Mohammed again agreed. Then he asked for his property to be returned. Mohammed said yes to that. Then the old Jew asked his Muslim friend what had happened to the chief of the tribe. "Killed." What had happened to their best poet? "Killed." What had happened to his best friend? "Killed." What had happened to one of the Jewish heroes? "Killed."

1692 Then the old Jew said, "Life holds no joy for me now that the best of my tribe are dead. I cannot bear to wait another moment to meet my loved ones." His Muslim friend struck off his head. When Abu Bakr heard the remark about the old Jew meeting his "loved ones" he said, "Yes, by Allah, he will meet them in Hell for eternity." Abu Bakr was to succeed Mohammed as leader of all Islam.

1693 To the victor go the spoils. Mohammed took the property, wives, and children of the Jews and divided them up among the Muslims. Mohammed got one fifth. He sent a Muslim with the female slaves to a nearby city where the women were sold for the pleasure of Muslim men. Mohammed invested the money from the sale of the slaves for horses and weapons.

1693 There was one last prize from the spoils of war for Mohammed. He took the most beautiful Jewess for his own pleasure after killing her husband and cousins and uncles. There is no record of her feelings as Mohammed had sex with his captive.

1696 In the Battle of the Trench it was Allah who had won the day. Allah had given the Muslim his strength and his will. No matter what the unbelievers did, Allah would triumph.

> 33:25 *And Allah drove back the unbelievers in their wrath, and they gained nothing by it. Allah aided the believers in the war, for Allah is strong and mighty.*

1697 Allah totally approved of killing the Jews and enslaving the women and children. It was good to give the Jews' property to the Muslim warriors. After all, Allah wanted it done and helped to do it.

> 33:26 *He brought down some of the People of the Book [the Jews] out of their fortresses to aid the confederates and to strike terror into their hearts. Some you killed, and others you took captive. He made you heirs of their land, their homes, and their possessions, and even gave you another land on which you had never before set foot. Allah has power over everything.*

1706 Some poetry of the Battle of the Trench:

> *We obeyed our prophet's orders.*
> *When he called for war we were the first to respond. When he called for violence we responded.*
> *When we saw battle we hastened. —Kab B. Malik*

> *Yearning sorrow reminds me of friends*
> *They have gone to Paradise.*

When he called them they answered.
All obeyed him utterly.
They gave no ground until they were all dead. —Hassan B. Thabit

THE KILLING OF THE JEW, ABU RAFI

1714 There was one piece of business that needed to be taken care of with respect to the Battle of the Trench. A Jew from Khaybar, Abu Rafi, had helped organize the confederation of tribes that attacked Mohammed. The two Arab tribes of Medina often competed with each other to please Mohammed. One tribe had assassinated the Jew who had written poetry criticizing Islam. The other tribe wanted to be able to assassinate someone, so tribe members suggested to Mohammed that they be allowed to kill Abu Rafi.

1714 Mohammed gave his permission and five assassins left for Khaybar. The only proviso was not to kill women or children. When they got to Khaybar it was night. They knocked at Abu Rafi's door, and his wife answered the knock. They told her they were Arabs looking to buy supplies, and she let them in. As soon as they entered, they bolted the door and shoved the wife aside. Although it was dark in the room, they could see Abu Rafi. They fell upon him with their swords as the wife screamed.

1715 After hacking at him, one of the men leaned over him and ran him through the stomach with a sword. The men fled, and one of them hurt himself falling. After they got away, they began to wonder if they had actually killed Abu Rafi or just badly wounded him. One of them was so bold as to suggest that he go back and mingle and see what the gathering crowd said. He heard a Jew say, "By the god of the Jews, he is dead!" The Arab had never heard sweeter words.

1716 Elated, the men headed back to report to the Apostle of Allah. After the report, the men fell to arguing over who had actually killed Abu Rafi. Mohammed demanded to see their swords. He examined them one by one and then pointed to the sword that had been the killing weapon. It still had food on it from the thrust to the stomach.

[*Ed.* The following, from Bukhari, is another version of this story.]

> B5,59,372 *Mohammed sent Abdullah Bin Atik and Abdullah Bin Utba with a group of men to Abu Rafi to kill him.*
>
> *They proceeded till they approached his castle, whereupon Abdullah Bin Atik said to them, "Wait here, and in the meantime I will go and see."*
>
> *Abdullah said later on, "I played a trick in order to enter the castle. By chance, they lost a donkey of theirs and came*

out carrying a flaming light to search for it. I was afraid that they would recognize me, so I covered my head and legs and pretended to answer the call to nature.

"The gatekeeper called, 'Whoever wants to come in should come in before I close the gate.'

"So I went in and hid myself in a stall of a donkey near the gate of the castle. They took their supper with Abu Rafi and had a chat till late at night. Then they went back to their homes. When the voices vanished and I no longer detected any movement, I came out. I had seen where the gate-keeper had kept the key of the castle in a hole in the wall. I took it and unlocked the gate of the castle, saying to myself, 'If these people should notice me, I will run away easily.'

"Then I locked all the doors of their houses from outside while they were inside and ascended to Abu Rafi by a staircase. I saw the house in complete darkness with its light off, and I could not know where the man was.

"So I called, 'O Abu Rafi!'

"He replied, 'Who is it?'

"I proceeded toward the voice and hit him. He cried loudly but my blow was futile. Then I came to him, pretending to help him, saying with a different tone of my voice, 'What is wrong with you, O Abu Rafi?'

"He said, 'Are you not surprised? Woe on your mother! A man has come to me and hit me with a sword!'

"So again I aimed at him and hit him, but the blow proved futile again, and on that Abu Rafi cried loudly and his wife got up. I came again and changed my voice as if I were a helper, and found Abu Rafi lying straight on his back, so I drove the sword into his belly and bent on it till I heard the sound of a bone break.

"Then I came out, filled with astonishment, and went to the staircase to descend, but I fell down from it and got my leg dislocated. I bandaged it and went to my companions limping. I said, 'Go and tell Allah's Apostle of this good news, but I will not leave this place till I hear the news of Abu Rafi's death.'

"When dawn broke, an announcer of death got over the wall and announced, 'I convey to you the news of Abu Rafi's death.'

"I got up and proceeded without feeling any pain till I caught up with my companions before they reached the Prophet to whom I conveyed the good news."

MORE BATTLES AND ROMANTIC TROUBLES

CHAPTER 19

47:33 Believers! Obey Allah and the messenger,
and do not let your effort be in vain.

THE ATTACK ON LIHYAN

1718 A few months after the annihilation of the last Jews of Medina, Mohammed led his troops on an attack upon the Arabs of Lihyan. They moved at a rapid pace but, when they arrived, the Lihyan tribe was high in the mountains and fortified. They had been warned. He headed south with two hundred riders toward Mecca just for the psychological pressure. Then they headed back to Medina. War is deceit.

THE ATTACK ON DHU QARAD

1720 Mohammed had been back in Medina only a few days when the Ghatafan Arabs raided Mohammed's camel pasture. They killed the Muslim herder and left with his wife and the camels. A rider came and told Mohammed and the chase was on. A small, quick posse was sent out ahead of a larger army. The posse was to make contact and harass the Ghatafans, and the army would come up and crush them.

1721 The army never engaged the Ghatafans, but the posse did manage to kill two of them and get one of their own killed. A few camels were recovered and they all went back to Medina.

THE RAID ON THE MUSTALIQ TRIBE

1725 Mohammed heard that the Arab tribe, the Mustaliqs, were gathering against him. So he set out with his army to oppose them. He contacted them at a watering hole and combat started. Islam was victorious and the Mustaliqs and their women, children, and goods were taken as spoils of war and distributed to the fighters. Only one Muslim was killed and that was by mistake by another Muslim.

> M19,4292 *I [Ibn Aun] wrote to Nafi inquiring from him wheth-*
> *er it was necessary to extend to the disbelievers an invitation to*
> *accept Islam before attacking them in fight. He wrote in reply to*

me that it was necessary in the early days of Islam. The Messenger of Allah made a raid upon Banu Mustaliq while they were unaware and their cattle were having a drink at the water. He killed those who fought and imprisoned others. On that very day, he captured Al-Harith. Nafi said that this tradition was related to him by Umar who himself was among the raiding troops.

B5,59,459 *Entering the mosque, Ibn Muhairiz saw Abu Said and asked him whether coitus interruptus was sanctified by Allah.*

Abu Said said, "Accompanying Mohammed at the Battle of Banu Al-Mustaliq, we were rewarded with Arab captives, including several woman which were very sought after because celibacy had become quite a hardship. We had planned to practice coitus interruptus but felt that we should seek instruction first from Mohammed. [Ed. Pregnancy was undesirable in the slaves because it diminished their value on the market.]

"Mohammed said, however, 'It is better that you not interrupt copulation to prevent pregnancy, because if a soul is predestined to exist, then it will exist.'"

After the battle, a fight broke out between the original Immigrants of the Quraysh tribe and the Helpers of Medina. Although Islam tried to have no tribal differences, there were rivalries between the Immigrants and the Helpers.

1726 One of the Helpers and an Immigrant were at the water when one shoved the other and they fell to fighting. One called out for his allies, the Helpers, and the other yelled for his friends, the Immigrants. Both groups were professional killers and the insults started. One Helper, who was a leader, said, "What? The Immigrants dispute our authority, and they have come to outnumber us in our own city. The Quraysh bums are an example of the old saying, 'Feed a dog and it will devour you.' When we return to our town, the stronger will drive out the weaker."

1726 When this was reported back to Mohammed, Umar was standing there and said, "Tell Abbad to go and kill him." Mohammed was in a bind. "Then people will say that Mohammed will kill his own," he said. "No. Give orders to set off now." It was earlier than he usually set out. He had the Muslims walk on foot for a day and night until, when they stopped, they were completely exhausted and fell to sleep at once. Mohammed's strategy worked. The men were too tired to argue and fight. The next morning they got up and a forced march with all the captives and their livestock finally put them back in Medina.

1728 After they had been back in Medina only a short time, another of the Helpers, a man of authority, came to Mohammed and offered to kill the offending Helper for Mohammed. Mohammed said no, that it could all be worked out. He turned to Umar, who had suggested killing the man immediately and said, "Now what do you think? Had I killed him when everyone was angry it would have created civil war. Now his own offer to kill him." Umar replied that Mohammed was the better strategist. But the tension between the Helpers and the Immigrants was to fester and erupt later.

1729 The captives of the tribe of Mustaliq were parceled out as spoils of war and ransom prices set upon their heads. If no one paid the ransoms, they were treated as spoils of war and slaves. One of them was a beautiful woman with a high price on her head. She came to Mohammed and asked him to see if the price could be reduced. Mohammed had a better idea. He would pay the ransom for the beautiful woman, and she could become his wife—in spite of the fact that she was already married. [The Koran gave permission for sex with married captives.] It was a deal. Mohammed paid the ransom, and the beautiful woman became wife number seven.

1729 A side effect of this marriage was that the captives were now related to Mohammed's wife, so they were all released without ransom.

THE LIE

When Mohammed went on his missions to attack and kill those who resisted Islam, he took one of his wives with him. Which one got to go was determined by lots. Mohammed took Aisha with him to the battle against the Mustaliqs. At the time of this expedition she was fifteen years old and the favorite of his seven wives.

1731 There was a problem in taking one of Mohammed's wives on an expedition and that was privacy. By now the veil had been proscribed for his wives so they could not be seen or heard. On trips, they rode in a tent-covered box that could be mounted on a camel's saddle. On the way back from the expedition Aisha had gone out in the morning to relieve herself. When she returned, she discovered that she had lost a necklace and went back to find it. Meanwhile the men in charge loaded the howdah on the camel and off they went without Aisha.

1732 When Aisha got back, the entire group had moved on. She wrapped herself in her smock and waited. They would return. Lo and behold, who should show up but a young warrior who had not spent the night in the camp. He put her on his camel and walked in search of the army, leading the camel with her on it. They could not catch the army, so the pair entered Medina, the young man leading the camel with Aisha on it.

1732 Here was a woman no one was even to speak with or see, and they had spent the day together all alone. Tongues began to wag, imaginations worked overtime, and gossip spread. Aisha fell ill and was bedridden for three weeks. While she was ill Mohammed spoke in the mosque about it. "Why are men worrying me about my family and saying false things about a man of whom I know nothing but good?"

1734 Tempers flared and men offered to kill the gossips. Something had to be done. Mohammed called in two men and asked their advice. The first said that both Aisha and the young man were innocent and the rumors were lies. Ali said, "Women are plentiful and can be exchanged one for another. Ask Aisha's slave girl about Aisha." So the slave girl was brought in, and Ali beat her severely and told her to tell Mohammed the truth about Aisha. The beaten slave told the prophet of Allah that she knew no ill of Aisha.

1735 Mohammed went to Aisha and told her what people were saying and that if she had done wrong to ask Allah for forgiveness. She told him she had done nothing to be forgiven for. Mohammed went into one of his trance states and Allah told him Aisha was innocent and the gossips should be flogged. This event determined the Koranic law about adultery. Adultery must have four witnesses. No witnesses means there is no adultery. Therefore, Aisha was innocent.

> 24:12 *Why did the believing men and women, when they heard this, not think better of their own people and say, "This is an obvious lie"? Why did they not bring four witnesses? And because they could not find any witnesses, they are surely liars in Allah's sight.*

1735 As for those who gossiped and lied:

> 24:4 *Those who make accusations against honorable women and are unable to produce four witnesses should be given eighty lashes. Thereafter, do not accept their testimony, for they are terrible sinners, except those who repent afterwards and live righteously.*

1736 But the scandal did not end there. One of those who were flogged was a poet. The young warrior who led Aisha's camel appeared in a poem written by the poet and was offended, so he took his sword and cut the poet badly. The poet and his friends managed to bind the young warrior and take him to Mohammed. Mohammed wanted all the trouble to go away. He gave the wounded poet a nice home and a Christian slave girl for sex as compensation for the sword blow.

THE TREATY OF AL HUDAYBIYA

CHAPTER 20

48.13 We have prepared a blazing Fire for these unbelievers
who do not believe in Allah and His Messenger.

1740 Mohammed decided to make a pilgrimage to Mecca. A difficult problem was how to do so peacefully. The state of affairs between Mohammed and the Meccans was violent. Mohammed called for all Muslims to go, but the Bedouin Arabs from around Medina refused his call. So he headed out with seven hundred men and seventy sacrificial camels. He and the others wore the white garments of the pilgrims so the Meccans would not suspect jihad.

1741 As they drew near to Mecca they learned the Quraysh had come out prepared for war and were blocking the way. So Mohammed took an alternate and difficult route to Mecca to try to avoid the armed Meccans. As the Muslims approached from the alternate route they stopped at Hudaybiya and waited for the Quraysh. One of the local clan leaders asked Mohammed what he wanted. He informed him that he wanted only to worship at the Kabah and had no intentions of making war.

1743 The Meccans were not going to let him enter the city, war or no war. They would not submit to Mohammed's wishes, and they would not lose face with the other Arabs. So Mohammed sent an envoy to the Meccans. At first he chose Umar, but since Uthman had kin in Mecca who could ensure his safety he sent him instead. (Both Umar and Uthman would be caliphs—supreme political and religious leaders—after Mohammed's death.)

1746 Uthman's mission into Mecca took longer than anyone thought it should, so the rumor started that he had been killed. Preparations for war started. Mohammed gathered the men to take a pledge that none would leave Mohammed without defending Islam. Then they heard the rumor was false; Uthman was alive.

1747 The Meccans sent a man out to make a treaty with Mohammed. Umar was furious that Mohammed would make a treaty with non-Muslims because it was demeaning to Islam. But Mohammed told him Allah would not let them lose; they would win over the Quraysh. Be patient.

1747 Mohammed said the treaty should acknowledge that he was the prophet of Allah. The Meccans insisted they would not sign anything like that. If they thought Mohammed was actually the prophet of Allah, there would be no problem anyway. So they drew up a treaty to the effect that there would be no war for ten years, there would be no hostilities, and no one could convert to Islam without a guardian's permission. In turn, the Muslims could come the following year and stay for three days in Mecca, but they could not enter that year.

1748 Many of the Muslims were depressed. Mohammed had promised they could enter Mecca. Now they could not. About this time a young Meccan man ran up wanting to join Mohammed, but his father had forbidden him. Even though the young man pleaded for protection as his father took him away, Mohammed made no protest. This depressed the Muslims even more. Mohammed counseled patience to all including the young man.

1748 Before they left, they sacrificed the camels, shaved their heads, and performed as many of the rituals as they could without getting into Mecca.

1749 On the way back to Medina, Mohammed added to the Koran the sura called "Victory" about the treaty. The desert Arabs who had not joined him on the pilgrimage would not get any war treasure in future battles.

> 48:15 *Those who lagged behind will say, when you go to take the spoils of war, "Let us follow you." They wish to change the word [the rules of how to divide the spoils of war] of Allah. Say: You will not follow us. Allah has already declared this. They will say, "No, you are jealous of us." No, they understand little.*

1750 There is a promise of war:

> 48:16 *Say to those desert Arabs who were left behind, "You will be called to fight against a people of mighty strength. You will fight until they submit. If you obey, Allah will give you a goodly reward, but if you turn back, as you turned back before, He will punish you with a grievous penalty."*

1750 Mohammed regarded the treaty with the Meccans as an oath to Allah and a victory for Islam. The government of Mecca had dealt with Mohammed as an independent political power. Many more Arabs were attracted to the religion of Islam now that it was powerful.

> B4,53,406 *While in Siffin, Sahl arose and scolded the people saying, "Brothers, accept blame. We stood alongside of Mohammed at Hudaybiya. We would have fought if we had been asked to."*

Then Umar came to Mohammed and questioned him, "Mohammed, are we not right and our enemies wrong?"

"Yes," Mohammed said.

Umar asked, "Do not our slain soldiers reside in Paradise while theirs burn in Hell?"

Mohammed said, "Yes."

Exasperated, Umar asked, "Then why should we accept a bad treaty that limits Islam! Will this treaty last until Allah judges between the believers and the non-believers?"

Mohammed said, "Umar, I am the prophet of Allah. Allah will never diminish me."

Umar then went to Abu Bakr and repeated the concerns he expressed to Mohammed. Abu Bakr said to him, "Mohammed is the prophet of Allah and Allah will never diminish him." The Victory, sura 48, of the Koran was then revealed to Mohammed who recited it in its entirety to Umar.

Umar then asked, "Mohammed, was the treaty of Hudaybiya really a victory for Islam?"

Mohammed said, "Yes."

THE FIRST DHIMMIS

CHAPTER 21

58:20 Those who oppose Allah and His Messenger will be laid low.

[Ed.: A *dhimmi* is a non-Muslim who is a second-class citizen in an Islamic country. There are many legal restrictions on dhimmis, such as not being able to testify against a Muslim. In addition, they must pay a special tax, *jizya,* which can be as high as 50 percent. The wealth of Islam came from the tax on the dhimmis.]

KHAYBAR

I756 After the treaty of Hudaybiya, Mohammed stayed in Medina for about two months before he collected his army and marched to Khaybar, a community of wealthy Jewish farmers who lived in a village of separate forts about a hundred miles from Medina.

> B4,52,41 *I asked Allah's Apostle, "O Allah's Apostle! What is the best deed?"*
> *He replied, "To offer the prayers at their early stated fixed times."*
> *I asked, "What is next in goodness?"*
> *He replied, "To be good and dutiful to your parents."*
> *I further asked, "What is next in goodness?"*
> *He replied, "To participate in jihad in Allah's Cause."*
> *I did not ask Allah's Apostle anymore, and if I had asked him more, he would have told me more.*

I757 When Mohammed raided a people, he waited until the morning. If he heard the call to prayer, which meant the people were Muslims, he would not attack but if there was no Muslim call to prayer he attacked. When he rode up with his army, workers were coming out to work in the fields. When they saw Mohammed and his army, they fled. Mohammed said, "Allah Akbar! Khaybar is destroyed. When we arrive in a people's square, it is a bad morning for those who have been warned."

> M19,4437 *The Messenger of Allah raided Khaybar. One morning we offered prayers in the darkness of early dawn near Khaybar. Then the Messenger of Allah mounted his horse. Abu Talha*

mounted his and I mounted behind Abu Talha on the same horse. The Prophet of Allah rode through the streets of Khaybar and I rode so close to him that my knee touched the thigh of the Prophet of Allah. The wrapper got aside from his thigh, and I could see its whiteness[1].

When he entered the town, he said, "Allah Akbar! Khaybar shall face destruction. When we descend in the city-square of a people, it is a bad day for them who have been warned and have not taken heed." He said these words thrice.

The people of the town had just come out from their houses to go about their jobs. They said, in surprise, "Mohammed has come."

We captured Khaybar by force.

1757 When the Ghatafan Arabs heard that Mohammed was going to attack Khaybar, they thought to confront him there. However, as they left they heard that their homes might be attacked and so they returned for security of their own property.

M31,5917 *Suhail reported on the authority of Abu Huraira that Allah's Messenger said on the Day of Khaybar, "I shall certainly give this standard in the hand of one who loves Allah and his Messenger and Allah will grant victory at his hand."*

Umar said, "Never did I cherish for leadership but on that day. I came before him with the hope that I may be called for this."

But Allah's Messenger called Ali, and he conferred this honor upon him and said, "Proceed on and do not look about until Allah grants you victory."

Ali went on a bit and then halted and did not look about and then said in a loud voice, "Allah's Messenger, on what issue should I fight with the people?"

Thereupon the Prophet said, "Fight with them until they bear testimony to the fact that there is no god but Allah and Mohammed is his Messenger, and when they do that, their blood and their riches are inviolable from your hands but what is justified by law and their reckoning is with Allah."

M19,4450 *When we reached Khaybar, its king named Marhab advanced, brandishing his sword and chanting:*

"Khaybar knows that I am Marhab,
"A fully armed, and well tried warrior
"When the war comes spreading its flames."
My uncle, Amir, came out to combat with him, saying:

---

1. References to Mohammed's whiteness are common in the Hadith.

> "*Khaybar certainly knows that I am Amir,*
> "*A fully armed veteran who plunges into battles.*"
> They exchanged blows. *Marhab's sword struck the shield of Amir who bent forward to attack his opponent from below, but his sword recoiled upon him and cut the main artery in his forearm which caused his death.*
>
> Salama said, "*I came out and heard some people among the Companions of the Holy Prophet saying: Amir's deed has gone waste; he has killed himself.*"
>
> So I [narrated by Ibn Salama's father] came to the Holy Prophet weeping and I said, "*Messenger of Allah. Amir's deed has gone waste.*"
>
> The Messenger said, "*Who passed this remark?*"
>
> I said, "*Some of your Companions.*"
>
> Mohammed said, "*He who has passed that remark has told a lie; for Amir there is a double reward.*" *Then he sent me to Ali, who had sore eyes, and said, "I will give the banner to a man who loves Allah and His Messenger or whom Allah and His Messenger love.*"
>
> So I went to Ali and brought him, and he had sore eyes, and I took him to the Messenger of Allah, who applied his saliva to his eyes and he got well. The Messenger of Allah gave him the banner and Ali went to meet Marhab in single combat.
>
> Marhab advanced chanting:
> "*Khaybar knows certainly that I am Marhab,*
> "*A fully armed and well tried valorous warrior hero*
> "*When war comes spreading its flames.*"
> Ali chanted in reply:
> "*I am the one whose mother named him Haidar,*
> "*I am like a lion of the forest with a terror-striking countenance.*
> "*I give my opponents the measure of sandara in exchange for sa'* [i.e., return their attack with one that is much more fierce]."
> Ali struck at the head of Mirhab and killed him, so the capture of Khaybar was due to him.

1758 Mohammed seized the forts one at a time. Among the captives was a beautiful Jewess named Safiyah. Mohammed took her for his sexual pleasure. One of his men had first chosen her for his own slave of pleasure, but Mohammed traded him two of her cousins for Safiyah. Mohammed always got first choice of the spoils of war and the women.

1759 On the occasion of Khaybar, Mohammed put forth new orders about forcing sex with captive women. If the woman was pregnant she was not to be used for sex until after the birth of the child. Nor were any women to be used for sex who were unclean with regard to Muslim laws about menstruation.

1759 One of the Muslim jihadists came to Mohammed to complain that he had received no spoils of war. Mohammed explained that there was none left to give him but held out hope that the next fort would be the richest in food. Sure enough, the next day Allah captured a rich Jewish fort and the man got his treasure.

> B2,14,68 *During the night Mohammed said the Fajr prayer, mounted his beast, and said, "God is great! Khaybar is destroyed! When we ride against a nation that has ignored our warning, they are in for the most terrible morning."*
>
> *As the people emerged from the city and saw our forces, they screamed the warning, "Mohammed and his army are here."*
>
> *Mohammed crushed them, killing their warriors and seizing their women and children. Dihya Al-Kalbi took Safiyah, although she was later given to Mohammed, who married her and gave Safiyah her freedom from slavery as a wedding present.*

1764 Mohammed knew there was a large treasure hidden somewhere in Khaybar so he brought forth the Jew he thought knew the most about it and questioned him. This Jew was Kinana, the husband of Safiyah, Mohammed's soon-to-be new bride. Kinana denied any knowledge. But another Jew said he had seen the man around one of the old ruins. The search was made, and a great deal of the treasure was found but not all of it. Mohammed told one of his men, "Torture the Jew until you extract what he has." So the Jew was staked on the ground and a small fire built on his chest to get him to talk. The man was nearly dead but would not talk, so Mohammed had him released and taken to one of his men whose brother had been killed in the fight, and the Muslim got the pleasure of cutting the tortured Jew's head off.

1760 When one fort had fallen, Bilal, Mohammed's freed black slave, brought Safiyah and another beautiful woman to Mohammed. He brought them past the dead and dying Jewish defenders, including their husbands. The woman with Safiyah began to shriek and pour dust on her head. Mohammed said to Bilal, "Take this she-devil away from me." Then he said to Bilal, "Had you no compassion, Bilal, when you brought the two women past their dead husbands?"

1764 The Jews of Khaybar were Mohammed's first dhimmis. After the best of the goods were taken from the Jews, Mohammed left them to work the land. His men knew nothing about farming and the Jews were skilled at it. So the Jews worked the land and gave Mohammed half their profits.

M10,3762 *Allah's Messenger returned the date-palms of Khaybar and its land to the Jews of Khaybar on the condition that they should work with their own wealth, seeds, and implements and give half of the yield to Allah's Messenger.*

I765 When the killing and capturing were done, the men rested. The next night a Jewess named Zaynab prepared the evening meal of roast lamb for Mohammed. She asked what was Mohammed's favorite joint and learned that it was the shoulder. She poisoned that joint and served the lamb to Mohammed and his companions. He tasted the meat and spit it out. It did not taste right, but another of his men wolfed down some of the lamb, fell ill, and died. Mohammed called her up and asked for an explanation. She told him he had killed her kin. If he was a king he would die from the poison and if he was a prophet it would not harm him, as he would know.

B4,53,394 *When Khaybar was conquered, a roasted poisoned sheep was presented to the Prophet as a gift by the Jews. The Prophet ordered, "Let all the Jews who have been here be assembled before me." The Jews were collected and the Prophet said to them, "I am going to ask you a question. Will you tell the truth?"*
They said, "Yes."
The Prophet asked, "Who is your father?"
They replied, "So-and-so."
He said, "You have told a lie; your father is so-and-so."
They said, "You are right."
He said, "Will you now tell me the truth, if I ask you about something?"
They replied, "Yes, O Mohammed; and if we should tell a lie, you can realize our lie as you have done regarding our father."
On that he asked, "Who are the people of the Hell Fire?"
They said, "We shall remain in the Hell Fire for a short period, and after that you will replace us."
The Prophet said, "You may be cursed and humiliated in it! By Allah, we shall never replace you in it."
Then he asked, "Will you now tell me the truth if I ask you a question?"
They said, "Yes, O Mohammed."
He asked, "Have you poisoned this sheep?"
They said, "Yes."
He asked, "What made you do so?"
They said, "We wanted to know if you were a liar in which case we would get rid of you, and if you are a prophet then the poison would not harm you."

1765 On the way back to Medina, one of Mohammed's slaves was removing Mohammed's saddle when a stray arrow hit and killed him. The Muslims congratulated him for dying a martyr. Mohammed said the slave would burn in Hell, since the cloak he was wearing had come from the spoils of war and he had stolen it. It was Allah's pleasure for the Muslims to take property in jihad, but if a Muslim stole any of the spoils before it was divided he would burn in Hell.

> B8,78,698 *We fought alongside Mohammed at the Battle of Khaybar, and although we did not receive any gold or silver as spoils of war, we did get miscellaneous property like clothes. However, a tribesman of the Bani Ad-Dubaib, Zaid, gave Mohammed a slave named Midam.*
>
> *In the Al-Qura valley, Midam was killed by an arrow shot by an unknown person. Some people said, "Congratulations to Midam for getting to Paradise."*
>
> *Mohammed cried, "No, Midam is not going to Paradise. By Allah, the sheet that he stole from the Khaybar spoils of war is burning over him in Hell." When the people heard what Mohammed had to say, one man returned a couple of leather straps that he had taken from the spoils of war. Mohammed said to him, "One strap of fire or two straps of fire for you."*

1766 On the way back Mohammed had one of the Muslim women prepare Safiyah (she was the Jewess he had picked for his pleasure) for her wedding night with Mohammed. That night one of his men marched around his tent for the whole night with his sword. The next morning Mohammed asked what he was doing and the man replied, "I was afraid for you because of the woman. You have killed her father, her husband, and her kin, so I was afraid for you on her account." Mohammed blessed him.

1770 While Mohammed was besieging Khaybar, a shepherd who worked for a Jew came over and asked him about Islam. The shepherd decided to become a Muslim and then asked Mohammed what to do about the sheep. Mohammed told him to send them back to their owner. The shepherd joined the raiders and was killed that day without ever praying a single prayer. Still, he went straight to heaven as a martyr. Mohammed said the shepherd now had two *houris*[1] for wives in heaven. Mohammed said that, when a martyr is slain, his new wives pet him and wipe the dust from his face and say, "May Allah put dust on the face of the man who put dust on your face and slay him who slew you."

---

1. Virgins of pleasure in Islamic heaven.

B8,77,603 *We witnessed along with Allah's Apostle the Khaybar campaign. Allah's Apostle told his companions about a man who claimed to be a Muslim, "This man is from the people of the Fire [Zoroastrian]."*

When the battle started, the man fought very bravely and received a great number of wounds and got crippled. On that, a man from among the companions of the Prophet came and said, "O Allah's Apostle! Do you know what the man you described as of the people of the Fire has done? He has fought very bravely for Allah's Cause, and he has received many wounds."

The Prophet said, "But he is indeed one of the people of the Fire."

Some of the Muslims were about to have some doubt about that statement. So while the man was in that state, the pain caused by the wounds troubled him so much that he put his hand into his quiver and took out an arrow and committed suicide with it. Off went some men from among the Muslims to Allah's Apostle and said, "O Allah's Apostle! Allah has made your statement true. So-and-so has committed suicide."

Allah's Apostle said, "O Bilal! Get up and announce in public: None will enter Paradise but a believer, and Allah may support Islam with a wicked man."

B9,83,29 *We went out with the Prophet to Khaybar. A man from the companions said, "O Amir! Let us hear some of your camel-driving songs." So he sang some of them [a lyric in harmony with the camels' walk].*

The Prophet said, "Who is the driver of these camels?"

They said, "Amir."

The Prophet said, "May Allah bestow His Mercy on him!"

The people said, "O Allah's Apostle! Would that you let us enjoy his company longer!" Then Amir was killed the following morning. The people said, "The good deeds of Amir are lost as he has killed himself."

I returned at the time while they were talking about that. I went to the Prophet and said, "O Allah's Prophet! Let my father be sacrificed for you! The people claim that Amir's good deeds are lost."

The Prophet said, "Whoever says so is a liar, for Amir will have a double reward as he exerted himself to obey Allah and fought in Allah's Cause. No other way of killing would have granted him greater reward."

1770 A Meccan named Al Hajjaj became a Muslim and took part in the capture of Khaybar. After the conquest he asked Mohammed's permission to go to Mecca and finish up his affairs and collect his debts. He then asked Mohammed if he could tell lies to get his money. The prophet of Allah said, "Tell them." So he set out for Mecca. When he got there the Meccans were asking for news from Khaybar. They did not know that the man had converted and so trusted him. He told them the Muslims had lost and that Mohammed had been captured. He said the Jews of Khaybar were going to bring Mohammed to Mecca so they could kill him.

1771 The Meccans were elated. He then asked them to help him collect his debts so he could return to Khaybar and profit from the confusion there. In good spirits they helped him collect the debts. He had been gone three days when they found out the truth of Khaybar and the fact that he was now a Muslim.

THE DIVISION OF THE TREASURE OF THE JEWS

1774 There was a total of eighteen-hundred people who divided up the wealth taken from the Jews of Khaybar. A cavalry man got three shares; a foot soldier got one share. Mohammed appointed eighteen chiefs to divide the loot. Mohammed got his fifth before it was distributed.

> B5,59,537 *On the day of Khaybar, Allah's Apostle divided the spoils of war of Khaybar with the ratio of two shares for the horse and one share for the foot soldier.*

FADAK

1777 The Jews of Fadak panicked when they saw what Mohammed did to Khaybar. They would be next, so they surrendered to Mohammed without a fight. Since there was no battle Mohammed got 100 percent of their goods, and they worked the land and gave half to Mohammed each year. They became dhimmis like those of Khaybar.

COLLECTING THE TAXES OF KHAYBAR

1778 The first tax collector of Khaybar was killed after one year and a new man was appointed. The new tax collector was killed as well. He was found in a pool of water with a broken neck, and there was no proof of who killed him. His relatives went to Mohammed and asked for blood money and revenge. When Mohammed asked them who should pay they did not know. He then asked if they would accept fifty oaths from the Jews that they were innocent? They said, "The oath of Jews is worthless. Their infidelity is so great that they are habitual liars." Mohammed resolved the issue by paying the blood money himself to the relatives.

1779 When Mohammed lay dying, his last words were that neither Jew nor Christian should remain in Arabia. When Umar became caliph he expelled all Jews and Christians, including those of Khaybar.

THE WINNING OF MECCA

CHAPTER 22

*61.11 Believe in Allah and His messenger and fight valiantly
for Allah's cause [jihad] with both your wealth and your
lives. It would be better for you, if you only knew it!*

THE NINTH WIFE

M383 Mohammed took his ninth wife, Um Habiba, the daughter of Abu Sufyan.

THE PILGRIMAGE

I789 After returning from Khaybar, Mohammed sent out many raiding parties and expeditions. Seven years after Mohammed moved to Medina and one year after the treaty of Hudaybiya, Mohammed led the Muslims on a pilgrimage to Mecca. While there he kissed one of the stones of the Kabah and trotted around it. When he got to the corner with the Black Stone, he walked up and kissed it. He did this for three circuits of the Kabah.

I789 As Mohammed entered Mecca, the man leading his camel said this poetry:

> *Get out of his way, unbelievers, make way.*
> *I know Allah's truth in accepting it.*
> *We will fight you about its interpretation*
> *As we have fought you about its revelation.*
> *We will cut off your head and remove friend from friend.*

I790 After his three-day stay, the Quraysh asked him to leave per the treaty. He asked to stay and have a wedding feast to which he would invite the Quraysh. The Quraysh refused and asked him to leave. He left.

THE RAID ON MUTA

B4,52,65 *A man came to the Prophet and asked, "A man fights
for the spoils of war; another fights for fame; and a third fights for
showing off; which of them fights in Allah's Cause?"*

> *The Prophet said, "He who fights that Allah's Word (Islam)*
> *should be superior fights in Allah's Cause."*

1791 Mohammed sent an army of three thousand to Muta soon after his return from Mecca. Muta was north of Medina, near Syria. When the Muslims got there they found a large army of Byzantines. The jihadists paused for two days of discussion. They had not been sent there to do battle with a professional army. What should they do? Many wanted to send a letter back to Mohammed and explain the new situation. If he wanted them to attack, so be it. If he wanted to send reinforcements that would be good. But one of them said, "Men, you are complaining of what you came here to do. Die as martyrs. Islam does not fight with numbers or strength but with Islam. Come on! We have only two prospects. Death or martyrdom; both are fine. Let us go forward!"

1796 The Muslims were cut to ribbons. The Christian Byzantines were professionals and superior in numbers. They were not Meccan merchants.

1796 Mohammed said that all three of the Muslim commanders went to heaven on beds of gold. But the final commander's bed turned away slightly as it approached heaven because he had paused before heading into destruction. He was not as complete a martyr. But Mohammed wept for all the dead. This was unusual as he had forbidden excessive mourning for those who died in jihad.

> B4,52,59 *Allah's Apostle said, "By Him in Whose Hands my*
> *soul is! Whoever is wounded in Allah's Cause...and Allah knows*
> *well who gets wounded in His Cause...will come on the Day of*
> *Resurrection with his wound having the color of blood but the*
> *scent of musk."*

1798 The toughness of the Muslims who remained behind in Medina was shown when they scorned the returning fighters. They threw dirt at them and said, "You are runaways. You fled from the way of Allah. You fled from jihad." Poetry was written to the effect that the men kept their distance from the Byzantine army and were afraid of death. They loved life too much and feared death.

MECCA CONQUERED

1803 At the treaty of Hudaybiya it was agreed that the Meccans and Mohammed could make alliances between themselves and other tribes. There were two different Arab tribes, one allied with the Meccans and the other allied with Mohammed. As tribes are prone to do, one tribe perpetrated a killing and the other retaliated. The situation was then escalated by the Quraysh of Mecca when they came to the aid of their ally. Naturally, the opposing tribe entreated Mohammed to take on the cause of his ally and punish the Quraysh.

1807 When the chief of the tribe allied with Mohammed was on his way back to Mecca, he met Abu Sufyan, a chief of the Quraysh. When Abu Sufyan asked where he was coming from, the chief lied. After they parted Abu Sufyan went back and looked at the chief's camel dung. Date pits. That meant the chief was returning from Medina. He had surely seen Mohammed. This was trouble as Mohammed never passed up a chance for war.

1807 So Abu Sufyan went to Medina as well. He stopped at the house of his daughter, who had submitted to Islam. Before he could step onto her sitting rug, she rolled it up. She explained that Mohammed had sat on the rug and she did not want her non-Muslim, unclean father sitting on it. He went to see Mohammed, but Mohammed would not see him. He then went to Abu Bakr and asked if he would speak with Mohammed for him. Abu Bakr would not do it. Next he went to Umar, but Umar threatened him. So finally he went to Ali. Ali would not help either, so he returned to Mecca and reported to the Quraysh.

1808 Mohammed prepared to fight in Allah's cause. He planned a surprise attack on Mecca.

1809 One of his fighters tried to sneak a letter to some Quraysh in Mecca, and the letter carrier was intercepted. (Mohammed always had excellent spies and up-to-date intelligence.) The fighter would have been executed except for the fact that he fought at Badr. All the veterans of Badr were revered. But the Koran said of this affair:

> 60:1 *O, you who believe, do not take My enemy and yours for friends by showing them kindness. They reject the truth that has come to you. They drive out the messengers and yourselves because you believe in Allah, your Lord. If you continue to fight for Allah's cause [jihad] and from a desire to please Me, would you show them kindness in private? I know best what you conceal and what you reveal. Whoever does this among you has already strayed from the right path.*

1811 Mohammed marched on Mecca with ten thousand men.

1813 The Muslims camped at a small town near Mecca. The Meccans needed to know Mohammed was going to enter their city. Many lives would be saved if the people would come out and seek protection. One of the fighters set out to find a local person to deliver the message and stumbled into Abu Sufyan, the Quraysh chief, who was determining for himself what was happening with this army.

1813 The Muslim fighter told Abu Sufyan that his only chance of survival was to come to Mohammed and ask for his protection. The Muslim was riding Mohammed's mule and Abu Sufyan mounted up behind him. As they approached a Muslim fire, they were challenged but, when the lookouts saw they were mounted on Mohammed's mule, they were allowed passage. As they passed Umar's fire, he challenged them. Umar immediately recognized Abu Sufyan and tried to kill him. The mule with its two riders and Umar raced for Mohammed's tent. They both got there at about the same time with Umar shouting for permission to kill the chief of the unbelievers. But the Muslim fighter told Mohammed he had given Abu Sufyan protection. Mohammed told both of them to come back in the morning.

1814 Abu Sufyan spent the night in the Muslim army camp and returned to Mohammed the next morning. Mohammed spoke, "Isn't it time for you to recognize that there is no god but Allah?" Abu answered, "I thought there was another god besides Allah, but he should have helped me." Mohammed replied, "Woe to you, Abu Sufyan, is it not time to recognize that I am Allah's apostle?" Abu Sufyan said, "As to that I have some doubt." He was told, "Submit and testify that there is no god but Allah and that Mohammed is his apostle before you lose your head!" So he did. [*Ed.* Abu Sufyan retained his rights as a commander and would later fight alongside Mohammed in battle.]

1814 Abu Sufyan was a proud man, and Mohammed gave him reason for it by promising that anyone who entered his house in Mecca would be safe and secure during the attacks. Also, all Meccans who stayed inside their own homes would be safe as well as those who stayed in the Kabah.

1814 Mohammed placed Abu Sufyan so he could see the army as it marched by. After he had seen the might of Mohammed's army, Abu Sufyan went ahead and announced to Mecca that Mohammed's army was coming. They were not to resist but to go into their houses, his house, or the Kabah and they would be safe.

1817 Mohammed's army entered Mecca from the north and from the south. One of the chiefs of the tribes of Medina said that, because this was war, sanctuary did not apply. When told of this, Mohammed had him replaced as a leader for that day with Ali.

1817 Some Meccans decided to resist Mohammed, but those few who did were quickly cut down. All in all, about thirteen of the Meccans were killed resisting Islam.

1819 Mohammed had told his commanders only to kill those who resisted; otherwise they were not to bother anyone except for those who had spoken against Mohammed. He then issued death warrants for all of those in Mecca who had resisted Islam. The list of those to be killed was:

- One of Mohammed's secretaries. He had said that Mohammed sometimes let him insert better speech when he was recording Mohammed's Koranic revelations, and this caused the secretary to lose faith.
- Two girls who had sung satires against Mohammed.
- A Muslim tax collector who had become an apostate (left Islam).
- A man who had insulted Mohammed.
- All artists and political figures who had opposed him.

1821 Mohammed went to the Kabah and rode around it seven times. Each time he went past the Black Stone, he touched it with his stick. Then he called for the key to the Kabah and entered. Inside was a carved wooden dove that he picked up and broke and threw out the door. There were also ritual objects and art of the various Arab faiths. Mohammed had them all burned and destroyed.

Mohammed's second order of business after assuming power was to destroy all religious art. The perfect pattern of Islam, aesthetics, and art was established.

Mohammed announced the end of all feuds, all revenge killings, and payment of blood money. The veneration of the ancestors was over.

T1642 Mohammed freed all the Meccans (since they had lost, they were all slaves). Then they gathered to pay homage to Mohammed and submit to Islam. The men came first; then came the women. One of the women was Hind who had mutilated Hamza's body on the battlefield at Uhud. He told her there were no gods except Allah and she agreed. Then he told her not to steal, commit adultery, or slander. She agreed to all of this. Then he told her not to kill her children. She replied, "I brought them up from babies, and you killed them on the day of Badr." He then told Umar to accept the women's pledge of loyalty, which involved touching their hands. Mohammed never touched women except those of his harem or those who were allowed him by law (women captured in combat could be used for sex).

1823 Even though revenge killing had been forbidden, one did occur. A brave man of Khirash's tribe had been killed in a raid. When Khirash found the killer in Mecca, he rushed at him and opened his belly so his guts spilled onto the floor. Mohammed told Khirash, "Stop the killing. There has been too much killing, even if there was a profit in it."

Mohammed paid the blood price to the man's relatives. Mohammed rebuked Khirash by saying, "Khirash is too prone to kill."

1824 The next day Mohammed said Mecca was made on the day of creation to be a holy city. It was not lawful to shed blood in Mecca or to cut down trees. Only Mohammed could kill in Mecca; no one else could do so. Those present were told to tell everyone else.

A NEW WIFE

M389 Mohammed took a tenth wife, Meimuna, age 26, a widow.

CLEANING UP THE DETAILS

CHAPTER 23

*64.12 So obey Allah and His messenger. But if you turn
your backs to them, Our messenger is not to blame, for
his duty is only to deliver Our warning clearly.*

KHALID'S ERROR

1833 Mohammed sent out troops to the surrounding areas of Mecca to invite the Arabs to submit to Islam. Among those he sent was Khalid.

1834 When the members of the tribe of Jadhima saw Khalid and his troops, they grabbed their weapons. Khalid said, "Lay down your arms for everyone has accepted Islam." But one of the Jadhima tribe called out, "Woe unto you, oh Jadhima. That is Khalid. If you lay down your arms, he will bind you and cut off your heads." But his tribal brothers insisted that would not happen and laid down their weapons.

1834 As soon as they disarmed, Khalid had them bound and put them to the sword.

1837 One of the bound men asked one of Khalid's men to lead him over to the women. He did so and the prisoner spoke a love poem to a woman. She went back with him as he was beheaded and wept and kissed him until they killed her as well.

1834 When this news reached Mohammed, he said, "O Allah, I am innocent before you of what Khalid has done."

1835 Mohammed sent Ali with blood money to pay for the deaths. He gave each relative the blood money and still had money left over. Ali asked if any more compensation was due and they said no. So he gave them the balance of what he had. He returned to Mohammed and told him what he had done. Mohammed said he had done well, and then he turned to the Kabah and raised his arms so that the whiteness of his armpits showed and repeated three times, "O Allah, I am innocent before you of what Khalid did."

KHALID'S DESTRUCTION OF THE NATIVE SHRINE

1840 Mohammed sent Khalid to an ancient temple near Mecca that was used by several tribes for worship. When Khalid got there he destroyed it completely.

THE BATTLE OF HUNAIN

1840 When Mohammed took Mecca, surrounding Arab tribes saw that he would be king of Arabia if he was not opposed. The Hawazin Arabs decided to oppose Mohammed under the leadership of Malik, who called for the advice of Durayd, a very old and experienced soldier. Durayd liked the location that Malik had chosen for the combat, but he wondered why he was hearing the sound of children and bleating sheep. Malik told him he was going to place the women, children, and livestock behind his men so they would not flee during battle. Durayd groaned and said, "You shepherd, do you think sheep will stop a man from running? If all goes well, nothing will help you except the sword and lance. If it goes badly, you will be disgraced with both family and property."

1841 Durayd said the allies were too few and were not from tribes of great warriors. He also criticized the battle array and Malik's strategy. But Malik was proud and refused the advice of an old man.

1842 Mohammed sent a spy to gather intelligence about the Arabs. When he got the information, he set about for jihad. He first borrowed armor and lances from a wealthy Meccan and then marched out with twelve thousand men.

> B4,52,52 *The Prophet said, "A single endeavor in Allah's Cause in the afternoon and in the forenoon is better than the world and whatever is in it."*

1845 When Mohammed's army descended into an area broad enough for combat they found the enemy prepared and waiting to attack.

> M5,2309 *We conquered Mecca, and then we went on an expedition to Hunain. The polytheists came, forming themselves into the best rows that I have seen. They first formed the rows of cavalry, then those of infantry, and then those of women behind them. Then there were formed the rows of sheep and goats and then of other animals. We were also people large in number, and our number had reached six thousand. And on one side Khalid Bin Walid was in charge of the cavalry. And our horses at once turned back from our rear. And we could hardly hold our own when our horses were exposed, and the Bedouins and the people whom we knew took to their heels.*

1845 The Muslim troops broke and ran. Mohammed stood in his stirrups and called out, "Where are you going? Come to me, the Apostle of Allah." Most of the men continued to retreat except his battle-hardened core troops who regrouped around him. A core of about a hundred men led the charge to turn the tide. They were steadfast. Mohammed looked at the carnage and said, "Now the oven is hot!"

> M19,4385 *I [Abbas] was in the company of the Messenger of Allah on the Day of Hunain. I and Abu Sufyan stuck to the Messenger of Allah, and we did not separate from him. And the Messenger of Allah was riding on his white mule.*
>
> *When the Muslims had an encounter with the disbelievers, the Muslims fled, falling back, but the Messenger of Allah began to spur his mule toward the disbelievers. I was holding the bridle of the mule of the Messenger of Allah, checking it from going very fast, and Abu Sufyan was holding the stirrup of the mule of the Messenger of Allah, who said, "Abbas, call out to the people of Al-Samura."*
>
> *I called out at the top of my voice: "Where are the people of Samura?" And by God, when they heard my voice, they came back to us as cows come back to their calves and said, "We are present, we are present!" They began to fight the infidels.*
>
> *Then there was a call to the Ansar. Those who called out to them shouted, "O Ansar [the Helpers]!"*
>
> *And the Messenger of Allah who was riding on his mule looked at their fight with his neck stretched forward and he said, "This is the time when the fight is raging hot." Then the Messenger of Allah took some pebbles and threw them in the face of the infidels. Then he said, "By the Lord of Mohammed, the infidels are defeated."*
>
> *I went round and saw that the battle was in the same condition in which I had seen it. By Allah, it remained in the same condition until he threw the pebbles. I continued to watch until I found that their force had been spent out and they began to retreat.*

1847 One of the Muslim women was near Mohammed and said about those who were retreating, "Kill those who flee just as you kill those who are attacking us."

1848 Two men were fighting, and a Muslim went over to help. In one sword stroke he cut off the hand of the nonbeliever, who then grabbed the Muslim by the throat and nearly killed him by strangulation. One more sword stroke finished him off. After the battle he went back and found that the man he had killed had already been stripped of his armor and weapons. No spoils of war. So he went to Mohammed and complained of his loss. Another Muslim admitted that he had taken the wealth of the man and that the man who killed him should be paid with his share of the distributed wealth. Abu Bakr, Mohammed's first in command, said, "No, by Allah, he shall not be paid from the general distribution. Are you going to make one of the lions of Allah who fought for Islam ask for shares? No, return the spoils to the one who killed him!" Mohammed confirmed this judgment, and the fighter took the spoils of war and sold it and bought his first real estate, a small palm-grove. But that was a small yield; one Muslim took the spoils of twenty men.

> B4,53,370 *During the Battle of Hunain, I [Abu Qatada] was in the company of Mohammed. After the battle was joined, the Muslim army had begun to retreat when I saw a non-Muslim attacking a Muslim. I attacked him from behind and dealt him a mortal blow, though he almost killed me before he expired.*
>
> *Following Umar, I asked him: "Why are the people fleeing?"*
> *"It is the will of Allah," he said.*
> *When the soldiers returned, Mohammed said, "Anyone who can prove that he killed an enemy soldier may have the dead man's possessions."*
> *I rose and asked: "Who will be my witness?"*
> *Mohammed repeated, "Anyone who can prove that he killed an enemy soldier may have the dead man's possessions."*
> *I stood up again and asked: "Who will be my witness?"*
> *Mohammed announced for a third time his call for claims and for the third time I asked for a witness.*
> *Mohammed asked me, "Abu Qatada, what do you have to say?"*
> *After I told him the whole story, a man got up and said, "Mohammed, he is telling the truth. I have the dead man's possessions. Please compensate the man for me."*
> *Abu Bakr spoke up, "No, by Allah, Mohammed will not give you the spoils of war won by a warrior that fights on behalf of Allah and Mohammed."*
> *Mohammed said, "Abu Bakr is correct."*
> *So, Mohammed gave me the man's armor, which I sold. I bought a garden with the money I received for the armor. It was the first property I acquired after my conversion to Islam.*

I856 One of those captured was a woman, and they handled her roughly. She told them she was Mohammed's foster sister. They brought her in front of Mohammed and he asked for proof. She reminded him of a bite he had given her when she carried him. He remembered this and treated her well. She decided to return to her tribe and not become a Muslim. Mohammed gave her two slaves, one male and one female.

M19,4453 *On the Day of Hunain, Umm Sulaim took out a dagger she had in her possession. Abiu Talha saw her and said, "Messenger of Allah, this is Umm Sulaim. She is holding a dagger."*

The Messenger of Allah asked her, "Why are you holding this dagger?"

She said, "I took it up so that I may tear open the belly of a polytheist who comes near me."

The Messenger of Allah began to smile at these words.

She said, "Messenger of Allah, kill all those people—other than us—whom you have declared to be free on the day of the Conquest of Mecca. They embraced Islam because they were defeated at your hands and as such their Islam is not dependable."

The Messenger of Allah said, "Umm Sulaim, God is sufficient against the mischief of the polytheists and He will be kind to us so you need not carry this dagger."

I859 A poem of the battle:

Crushing the heads of the nonbelievers
Now choking them with bare hands
Now splitting their skulls with a sharp sword
Obedience to Allah and Mohammed.
We conquered with his flag and commission
A glorious life and authority that will not cease.
The day we trod down the unbelievers
We did not turn from the Prophet's orders.
In battle people only heard
The exhortations and smashing of skulls
By swords that severed the necks of warriors at a blow.
We left the slain cut to pieces.
'Tis Allah we please, not man. —Bin Mirdas

THE CAPTURE OF AL TAIF

I870 When Mohammed had finished at Hunain, he set out for Al Taif.

I872 On the way, he passed a walled house. Mohammed called out that, if the man did not come out of his house, the Muslims would tear down his wall. He would not come out and the Muslims tore down his wall.

B4,52,72 *Mohammed told us that Allah revealed to him that "any holy warrior killed will go to Paradise."*

Umar asked the prophet, "Is it true that Muslims killed in battle will go to Paradise, and non-Muslims who are killed in battle will go to Hell?"

Mohammed said, "Yes."

1872 They reached Al Taif and camped near its walls. Some Muslims were killed when arrows from the besieged city hit them, so they withdrew their camp. They fought for days just exchanging arrows with the city. Then the Muslims stormed the wall using a *testudo* (a roofed moveable structure) to avoid the arrows, but the defenders dropped hot iron on the roof of the testudo and set it ablaze. As the Muslims tried to escape, the defenders shot them; so Mohammed cut down their vineyards.

1874 Mohammed took stock of the situation. As he was doing so, one of the Muslim women came over and asked him if she could have the jewelry of one or two women of the tribe under siege. It so happened these women were well known for the fineness of their jewelry. Mohammed told her she might not get to wear the jewelry because he'd had a foreboding dream. They broke camp.

1874 One of the Muslims was very irritated. He had come for the sole purpose of getting a slave girl. This particular Arab tribe was noted for its intelligence and the Muslim wanted her to breed smart sons for him.

1877 On the way back from the siege of Al Taif, Mohammed stopped where many of the prisoners and livestock of the Hunain battle were kept. The elders of the defeated tribe reminded him that some of their tribe had been his foster kin. Mohammed asked them whether they wanted their livestock or their wives and children returned. Naturally, they said they wanted their families back.

1878 When the noon prayers were over, Mohammed asked if those who had the spoils of the Hunain battle would be willing to return the women and children. His oldest converts, the Helpers and the Immigrants, said yes. But those from a recently allied tribe said no. So Mohammed offered them six camels for each person if they would return them.

1878 From the lot of the women, Mohammed had chosen three as gifts of pleasure to his companions. He gave Ali one slave for sex and gave one each to Uthman and Umar too. So Mohammed gave slaves of pleasure to his two sons-in-law and father-in-law. Umar gave his sex slave to his son. It is not recorded if the women were returned to their mothers and fathers.

1878 One of the men had a female captive who was old, and he didn't want to give her up for six camels. He said she was of high standing in the tribe and was worth more. Another Muslim told him, "Let her go! Her mouth is cold, her breasts are flat, and she cannot conceive. Not only that, her husband will not care. Give her up." The man gave her up for the six camels, but later he still complained about it. He was told, "Shut up. It is not like you took her as a virgin or even a plump matron."

1879 One man was a chief whom Mohammed wanted for his influence. Mohammed sent word that he would give him a hundred camels and return his family if he would submit to Islam. The man did so.

1880 After Mohammed had returned the families, the Muslim fighters pressed him hard for the division of the livestock as the spoils of war. As a matter of fact, they pressed him so hard they shoved him against a thorn tree that tore off his mantle. That angered him, but he gave them all they wanted.

1885 All the new Muslims were receiving the spoils of war, but the Helpers had received nothing and they were angry. So one went and complained and Mohammed had them all gather.

1886 Mohammed praised Allah and then said, "O Helpers, what is this I hear of you? Do you think ill of me in your hearts? Did I not come to you when you were in error? You were poor, and now Allah has made you rich. You had many enemies, and now your hearts are softened." The Helpers replied, "Yes, you and Allah have been kind and generous." Then Mohammed said, "Had you wished, you could have said that I came to you when I was discredited and you believed me. I was deserted and you helped me. I was poor and you comforted me. And all of this would have been true. Are you disturbed because I have given good things to others to influence them to be Muslims? Are you not satisfied that others will take livestock away and you will take back the Apostle of Allah? By Allah, if it were not for the Immigrants, I would have become a Helper myself. If all men went in one direction and the Helpers went the other, I would go with the Helpers. May Allah have mercy on the Helpers."

1886 The men cried until tears ran off their beards. "We are satisfied with our share." And they left feeling grateful.

> M5,2303 *When on the Day of Hunain Allah conferred upon His Apostle the riches of the Hawazin without armed encounter, the Messenger of Allah set about distributing to some persons of Quraysh one hundred camels.*
>
> *Upon this the young people from the Ansar said, "May Allah grant pardon to the Messenger of Allah that he bestowed these camels upon the people of Quraysh, and he ignored us, whereas our swords are still dripping blood."*
>
> *Their statement was conveyed to the Messenger of Allah, and he sent someone to the Ansar and gathered them under a tent of leather. When they had assembled, the Messenger of Allah came to them and said, "What is this news that has reached me from you?"*

The wise people of the Ansar said, "Messenger of Allah, so far as the sensible among us are concerned they have said nothing, but we have among us persons of immature age. They said, 'May Allah grant pardon to the Messenger of Allah that he gave to the Quraysh and ignored us despite the fact that our swords are be-smeared with their blood.'"

Upon this the Messenger of Allah said, "I give at times materi-al gifts to persons who were quite recently in the state of unbelief, so that I may incline them to truth. Don't you feel delighted that people should go with riches, and you should go back to your homes with the Apostle of Allah? By Allah, that with which you would return is better than that with which they would return."

They said, "Yes, Messenger of Allah, we are pleased."

The Holy Prophet said, "You would find marked preference in conferring of the material gifts in future, so you should show pa-tience till you meet Allah and His Messenger in Paradise."

They said, "We would show patience."

THE AFFAIR OF THE POET

I888 A poet named Kab had satirized Mohammed. His brother wrote to him, saying Mohammed killed those who spoke against him. Those poets who could had escaped from Arabia. However, if Kab apologized and be-came a Muslim, all would be forgiven. Otherwise, he should flee.

I889 Kab wanted to live and remain in Arabia. Other friends also told him he was a dead man if he didn't leave or convert, so he wrote a poem praising Mohammed and repenting.

I889 Then Kab set out for Medina and went to the mosque and asked which man was Mohammed. Someone pointed him out. Kab went di-rectly to him after prayers and asked, "If Kab, the poet, came to you as a repentant Muslim, would you accept him?" Mohammed said he would. Then Kab said he was that man. Immediately one of the Helpers leapt up and asked permission to behead Kab. Mohammed told the Helpers to leave the man alone, as he was now a Muslim. A Muslim should never kill another Muslim.

MARY, THE COPTIC SLAVE OF PLEASURE

M425 Mohammed was given two Coptic (Egyptian Christian) slaves. One he gave to another Muslim but he kept Mary, fair of skin with curly hair. He did not move her into the harem but set her up in an apartment in another part of Medina. Mary provided something in sex that none of his wives could—a child, and it was a male child, Abraham. Mohammed doted on him.

M426 The harem was jealous. This non-Arab slave had given Mohammed his best gift. Then, while one of his wives, Hafsa, was away, Mohammed took Mary to her apartment in the harem. Hafsa returned and there was a scene. Mohammed tried to keep it quiet but the harem was incensed: a slave in one of their beds was an outrage and a scandal. The wives banded together, and it was a house of anger and coldness.

M427 Mohammed withdrew and swore he would not see his wives for a month and lived with Mary. Omar and Abu Bakr were appalled as Mohammed, their son-in-law, abandoned their daughters for a slave. Finally, Mohammed relented and said Gabriel had spoken well of Hafsa and he wanted the whole affair to be over.

The Koran:

> 66:1 *Why, O, Messenger, do you forbid yourself that which Allah has made lawful to you? Do you seek to please your wives? [Mohammed told Hafsa he would stop relations with Mary and then did not, but Hafsa was supposed to be quiet about the matter.] Allah is lenient and merciful. Allah has allowed you release from your oaths, and Allah is your master. He is knowing and wise.*
>
> 66:3 *When the Messenger confided a fact to one of his wives, and when she divulged it [Hafsa told Aisha (Mohammed's favorite wife) about Mary and the harem became embroiled in jealousy], Allah informed Mohammed of this [Mohammed learned of the problem in his harem], and he told her [Hafsa] part of it and withheld part. When Mohammed told her of it, she said, "Who told you this?" He said, "He who is knowing and wise told me."*
>
> 66:4 *"If you both [Hafsa and Aisha] turn in repentance to Allah, your hearts are already inclined to this, but if you conspire against the Messenger, then know that Allah is his protector, and Gabriel, and every just man among the faithful, and the angels are his helpers besides. Perhaps, if he [Mohammed] divorced you all, Allah would give him better wives than you—Muslims, believers, submissive, devout, penitent, obedient, observant of fasting, widows, and virgins."*

Abraham died about a year later.

THE RAID ON TABUK

I894 Mohammed decided to raid the Byzantines. Normally, he never let his men actually know where he was headed. He would announce a general destination and, after they were on the way, announce the actual place. But this raid was far away and the weather was very hot, so more complicated preparations needed to be made. The men began to prepare but with no enthusiasm due to the heat. Besides, it was time for harvest to begin, and they remembered the last combat with the Byzantines—they lost badly.

> B4,52,198 *When Mohammed planned an attack, he would use deceit to conceal his objective, the exception being the Battle of Tabuk, which was fought during extremely hot weather. Facing a long trek through the desert before attacking a formidable host, Mohammed told his army their destination and made clear their difficult situation.*

1894 When Mohammed asked one of his best men if he wanted to go, the man replied, "Would you allow me to stay? You know how much I love women and, when I see the Byzantine women, I don't know if I will be able to control myself." So Mohammed told him to stay, but the Koran had a comment:

> 9:49 *Some of them say to you, "Allow me to remain at home, and do not expose me to temptation." Have they not already fallen into temptation? Hell will surround the unbelievers.*

1895 There was much grumbling about the heat.

> 9:81 *Those who were left behind were delighted at sitting behind Allah's Messenger. They hated to strive and fight with their riches and their lives for Allah's cause [jihad] and said, "Do not go out in the heat." Say: The Fire of Hell is a fiercer heat. If they would only understand. Let them laugh a little for they will weep much in payment for their deeds.*

1896 Mohammed urged those who could to finance the jihad. Those with wealth did so. There were seven poor fighters who came to Mohammed and begged to go, but they had no mounts. Mohammed said he had no mounts and they left crying, but a Muslim gave them an old camel suitable only for carrying water and dates, and they went off with Mohammed.

1896 When Mohammed set off, there were many Muslims who were slow to leave or who came with misgivings. After the first camp, some of them returned to Medina. These were called *hypocrites.*

> 9:47 *If they had intended to go to war, they would have prepared for war. But Allah was opposed to their marching forth and held them back. It was said, "Sit at home with those who sit." If they had taken the field with you, they would not have added to your strength but would have*

hurried about among you, stirring up dissension. Some of you would have listened to them. Allah knows the evildoers.

1897 Mohammed left his son-in-law, Ali, behind to take care of Mohammed's family. After Mohammed was on the trail, some of the Medinans told Ali that Mohammed did not want to take him along because he was a burden and Mohammed didn't want him around. This angered Ali, so he grabbed his weapons, saddled his camel, and set out to catch Mohammed. When he caught up, Mohammed told him to go back. He said those men were liars, and he needed Ali to care for his family. Ali went back.

1901 As the journey went on, some men dropped out. Mohammed said of them, "Let them be. If there is any good in them, they will rejoin; if not, Allah has rid us of them."

1902 When they got to Tabuk, the people there paid the poll tax. By paying the per person tax, they gained immunity and Mohammed would not attack and kill them or rob their caravans.

1903 Mohammed sent Khalid to the fort of a Christian ruler. When the ruler and his brother rode out of their fort to inspect their cattle, Khalid killed the brother and captured the ruler. The Christian's robe was so beautiful that Khalid sent it to Mohammed. The Muslims admired it, but Mohammed said he preferred a rag from one of his martyrs. The ruler agreed to pay the poll tax to Islam, and Mohammed returned to Medina.

THE PUNISHMENT OF THE THREE

1908 When Mohammed returned to Medina there were many who had chosen not to go on jihad with him. Three drew his attention (the text is not clear exactly why), and he ordered them shunned. No one was to go to their houses or even speak to them. Many of those who stayed behind came to him and apologized, but Mohammed remained silent.

1909 In a small community, public shunning was socially crippling, and the three who were being punished were hurt. After forty days, even their wives were ordered to shun them.

> B6,60,199 *I heard Kab Bin Malik, who was one of the three who were forgiven, saying that he had never remained behind Allah's Apostle in any battle which he had fought except two—Tabuk and Badr. He added: I decided to tell the truth to Allah's Apostle in the forenoon, and scarcely did he return from a journey he made, except in the forenoon, he would go first to the mosque and offer a two-Rakat prayer. The Prophet forbade others to speak to me or to my two companions, but he did not prohibit speaking to any of those who had remained behind excepting us.*

So the people avoided speaking to us, and I stayed in that state till I could no longer bear it, and the only thing that worried me was that I might die and the Prophet would not offer the funeral prayer for me, or Allah's Apostle might die and I would be left in that social status among the people that nobody would speak to me or offer the funeral prayer for me. But Allah revealed His Forgiveness for us to the Prophet in the last third of the night while Allah's Apostle was with Um Salama. Um Salama sympathized with me and helped me in my disaster.

Allah's Apostle said, "O Um Salama! Kab has been forgiven!"

She said, "Shall I send someone to him to give him the good tidings?"

He said, "If you did so, the people would not let you sleep the rest of the night." So when the Prophet had offered the Fajr prayer, he announced Allah's Forgiveness for us. His face used to look as bright as a piece of the full moon whenever he was pleased.

When Allah revealed His Forgiveness for us, we were the three whose case had been deferred while the excuse presented by those who had apologized had been accepted. But when there were mentioned those who had told the Prophet lies and remained behind in the Battle of Tabuk and had given false excuses, they were described with the worst description one may be described with.

Allah said: "They will present their excuses to you when you return to them. Say: Present no excuses; we shall not believe you. Allah has already informed us of the true state of matters concerning you. Allah and His Apostle will observe your actions."

1913 On the fiftieth day of their shunning Mohammed announced that Allah had sent down forgiveness for the men who had slacked on their duty of jihad to Tabuk. So Mohammed did not chastise them; Allah did.

9:118 *Allah also turned in mercy to the three who were left behind. Their guilt caused them to feel that the earth, spacious as it is, constrained them. Their souls became so confined within them that they thought there was no refuge from Allah but in Him. Then He turned to them, in mercy, so that they might repent. Allah is constant and merciful. Believers, fear Allah, and be with those who are truthful.*

THAQIF SUBMITS TO ISLAM

1914 One of the men from Thaqif came to Mohammed to submit to Islam. When he went back to Thaqif, he announced his conversion from the top of his house. The men of Thaqif responded by shooting arrows at him and killing him. The natives of Thaqif were growing tired of the persecution and danger in not being a Muslim. As one said, "Our herds are not safe. We cannot go out without being cut off." So they decided to submit to Islam and gain peace.

I916 They sent a large delegation to Mohammed, which tried to negotiate with Mohammed. They wanted to wait three years before destroying their native religious objects, but Mohammed would have none of that. Finally, the best deal to be made was that Mohammed would send someone to destroy all the native religious objects so the members of Thaqif would not have to do the work themselves, as they loved their old religion.

ETERNAL JIHAD

> B,52,53 *Mohammed said, "Nobody who died and went to Paradise would want to return to life even if he were given the world and all its possessions, the exception being the martyr that recognized the moral superiority of giving one's life for Allah and who wished to return to life only to give it again."*
>
> *Mohammed said, "A single act of jihad in the afternoon or morning is greater than the entire world and everything in it. A place in Paradise, no matter how small, is greater than the entire world and everything in it. If a houri [a virgin of Paradise devoted to perfect sexual satisfaction] came from Paradise and revealed herself to man, she would fill the sky between heaven and earth with bright light and sweet aromas. The veil she wears is greater than the entire earth and everything in it."*

M448 After all the victories some Muslims said the days of fighting were over and even began to sell their arms. Mohammed forbade this, saying, "There shall not cease from the midst of my people a party engaged in fighting for the truth until the Antichrist appears." Jihad was therefore the normal state of affairs. Indeed, the Koran prepared the way for this:

> 9:122 *The faithful should not all go out together to fight. If a part of every troop remained behind, they could instruct themselves in their religion and warn their people when they return to them that they should guard against evil.*

ABU BAKR LEADS THE PILGRIMAGE

I919 Abu Bakr led the pilgrimage from Medina to Mecca. While they were in Mecca, major changes were made to the treaty of Hudaybiya, per the Koran. The treaty was only good for four more months.

> 9:1 *A declaration of immunity from Allah and His Messenger to the unbelievers with whom you have made a treaty: Travel freely in the land for*

four months, but know that you cannot escape Allah and that those who do not believe will be put to shame by Allah.

9:3 *Allah and His Messenger proclaimed to the people on the day of the greater pilgrimage: "Allah and His Messenger are free from any obligations with the unbelievers. If you repent to Allah, it will be better for you, but if you turn away, then know that you cannot escape Allah." Announce a painful punishment to those who do not believe.*

1920 After the four-month period, jihad would be declared upon those of the native religions unless they submitted to Islam.

9:5 *When the sacred months [by ancient Arab custom there were four months during which there was to be no violence] are passed, kill the unbelievers wherever you find them. Take them as captives, besiege them, and lie in wait for them with every kind of ambush. If they submit to Islam, observe prayer, and pay the poor tax, then let them go their way. Allah is gracious and merciful.*

1922 After this date those who practiced the old native religions of Arabia would no longer be able to come to Mecca for pilgrimage.

9:17 *It is not for the unbelievers to visit or maintain temples of Allah while they witness against their own souls to disbelief. Their work bears no fruit; they will abide in the Fire forever. Only he who believes in Allah and the Last Day should visit the mosques of Allah, observe regular prayer, and practice regular charity, and fear only Allah.*

Family, friends, wealth, businesses, and homes all had to be less important than Allah, Mohammed, and jihad.

9:24 *Say: If your fathers, and your sons, and your brothers, and your wives, and your kin-folks, and the wealth which you have gained, and the merchandise that you fear you will not sell, and the dwellings in which you delight—if all are dearer to you than Allah and His Messenger and efforts on His Path, then wait until Allah's command comes to pass. Allah does not guide the impious.*

1924 The non-Muslims were unclean and could not approach the Kabah. The money lost from their pilgrimages would be taken care of by Allah.

9:28 *O, believers, only the unbelievers are unclean. Do not let them come near the Sacred Temple after this year of theirs. If you fear poverty from the loss of their business [breaking commercial ties with the Meccans], Allah will enrich you from His abundance if He pleases. Allah is knowing and wise.*

1924 Jihad against the non-Muslims would result in a poll tax that would compensate for the lost pilgrimage incomes.

> 9:29 *Make war on those who have received the Scriptures [Jews and Christians] but do not believe in Allah or in the Last Day. They do not forbid what Allah and His Messenger have forbidden. The Christians and Jews do not follow the religion of truth until they submit and pay the poll tax [jizya], and they are humiliated.*

1924 The Koran then turned to the issue of the raid on the Byzantines at Tabuk. Muslims were required to answer the call to jihad. It was an obligation.

> 9:38 *O, believers, what possessed you that when it was said, "March forth in Allah's cause [jihad]," you clung heavily to the earth? Do you prefer the life of this world to the next? Little is the comfort of this life compared to the one that is to come. Unless you march forth, He will punish you with a grievous penalty, and He will put another in your place. You will not harm Him at all, for Allah has power over everything.*

1924 If the Byzantine raid had been short and produced easy war spoils, the Muslims would have joined readily, but instead they made excuses.

> 9:42 *Had there been a near advantage and a short journey, they would certainly have followed you, but the journey was too long for them. Yet they will swear by Allah saying, "If we only could have, we would surely have gone forth with you." They would destroy their own souls. Allah knows that they are surely lying.*

1924 A Muslim's duty was not to avoid fighting, either personally or with money.

> 9:44 *Those who believe in Allah and in the Last Day do not ask for exemption from fighting with their wealth and their lives. Allah knows those who fear Him.*

1926 Those who tried to avoid jihad were hypocrites, and the prophet was to struggle against them. They were bound for Hell.

> 9:73 *O, Prophet, strive hard against the unbelievers and the hypocrites, and be firm with them. Hell will be their dwelling place: A wretched journey.*

1927 In the past Mohammed had gone to the graves of some of the hypocrites and prayed, but a Muslim was not to pray for a non-Muslim or stand at his grave.

9:84 *Never pray over nor stand over the grave of anyone of them who dies because he did not believe in Allah and His Messenger and died in his wickedness.*

Those who believed in Allah and the apostle and entered jihad with their wealth and lives would prosper and enter Paradise. This was a promise from Allah.

9:88 *The Messenger and those who share his faith strive hard for their faith with their purses and lives. All good things await them. These are the ones who will prosper. Allah has made ready for them Gardens beneath which the rivers flow, where they will remain forever. This is the supreme felicity.*

9:111 *Allah has bought from the believers their lives and their wealth, and in return theirs is the Garden of Paradise. They will fight on the path of Allah so they slay and are slain. It is a promise binding on Him in truth through the Law, in the Gospel, and in the Koran, and who is more faithful to His promise than Allah? Rejoice, therefore, in the pledge that you have made, for this will be the great bliss.*

1932 Some poetry from this period:

Carrying horsemen accustomed to fighting warriors
And to smiting down brave foes
Never retreating, but always advancing
We came back with their leaders
And with their women and children also divided among the warriors
We inherited their houses when they were gone
And remained there as owners
When the Apostle brought us the truth.

THE DEPUTATIONS

1933 When Mohammed had taken Mecca and Tabuk, deputations began to come from other Arabs. They had been waiting to see how the conflict played out between the Quraysh and Mohammed. When Mohammed was victorious the Arabs came in groups and joined the winner.

110:1 *When the help of Allah and the victory arrive, and you see men entering the religion of Allah in ranks, then celebrate the praises of your Lord and pray for His forgiveness, for He is always ready to show mercy.*

Ishaq's biography goes on for some pages about the different tribes who came to submit to Islam. One interesting story that portrays the motives of some who joined is that of a Christian chief.

ADIY, THE CHRISTIAN

1947 No man disliked Mohammed more than Adiy. Seeing Mohammed rise in political power, he made plans to evacuate when Mohammed came with his warriors. Sure enough, the word came that Mohammed was near, and Adiy took his family and left for Syria. In his rush he left behind his niece. She was captured and then released to travel to find her Uncle Adiy. She advised him to join Mohammed, saying, "If he is a prophet, those who join early will have an advantage, and if he is a king you will not be shamed." So he went to see Mohammed.

1949 When Adiy met Mohammed he was impressed by him although he did not act like a king. Mohammed said, "The poverty of the Muslims might cause you to not want to join Islam, but, by Allah, there will soon be such a flood of wealth that people will not be able to handle it. You think that others have the power, but soon the castles of Babylon will be open to Islam." So Adiy became a Muslim.

THE KINGS OF HIMYAR

1956 The kings of Himyar wrote to Mohammed that they had submitted to Islam. Mohammed wrote back, "I received your message and am informed of your conversion to Islam and your killing non-Muslims. Allah has guided you. Send one fifth of the spoils of war, and tax the nonbelievers. Christians and Jews who do not convert must pay the poll tax."

THE BANU'L-HARITH ACCEPT ISLAM

1959 Mohammed sent Khalid to the people of Banu'l-Harith to give the tribe three days to accept Islam before he attacked it. So Khalid sent out riders to announce: "If you accept Islam you will be safe." The tribe accepted and Khalid taught everyone Islam.

1960 When the tribe members came to visit Mohammed, he said they were the men who, when driven away, pushed forward. Then he said, "If Khalid had not written that you accepted Islam, I would have thrown your heads beneath your feet."

1961 Mohammed then sent them back home with detailed religious instructions as well as the directive to send him one fifth of the spoils of war that were due him.

> B1,10,501 *Leaders from an Arab tribe came to Mohammed and said, "Our tribe is separated from you by distance and enemies, and we can only visit during the sacred months. Give us commandments so that we may bring them to our people."*

Mohammed said, "I command you to do four things, and I forbid you to do one. The things you must do are admit that there is but one god, Allah and Mohammed is His prophet; strictly follow rules governing prayer; pay taxes to support the needy; and, finally, give me one fifth of all spoils of war. The thing that you must not do is drink alcohol."

THE POOR TAX

1965 Mohammed sent out tax collectors to every part of Islam to collect the poor tax, the *zakat*.

MOHAMMED'S LAST YEAR

72.23 My only task is to convey Allah's truth and His message. Those who rebel against Allah and His apostle have the fire of Hell, and they will remain there forever!

THE FAREWELL PILGRIMAGE

1968 Ten years after entering Medina, Mohammed made what was to be his last pilgrimage to Mecca, where he made his farewell address. He told the Muslims that usury was abolished; Allah would judge them and their works; all the blood shed before Islam was to be left unavenged; and the lunar calendar was the sacred calendar and was not to be adjusted with respect to the solar calendar.

1969 He also told them men had rights over their wives and women had rights over their husbands. The wives were never to commit adultery or act in a sexual manner toward others. If they did, they were to be put in separate rooms and beaten lightly. If they refrained from what was forbidden, they had the right to food and clothing. Men were to lay injunctions on women lightly for they were prisoners of men and had no control over their persons.

M473 He said to feed and clothe their slaves well.

1969 He said every Muslim was a Muslim's brother and to take from a brother only what he willingly gave.

1970 Then Mohammed led the Muslims through the rituals of the pilgrimage.

THE FINAL STATE OF CHRISTIANS AND JEWS

M453 When Mohammed first was preaching, his religion was Arabian. Then during the last phase in Mecca, he made Allah the same as Jehovah and introduced Jewish elements into his faith. When Mohammed moved to Medina, he argued with the Jews when they denied his status as a prophet in the line of the Jews. He then annihilated the Jews and said no more about his Jewish roots. In his last statement regarding them, Jews and Christians became perpetual second-class citizens, dhimmis:

9:29 *Make war on those who have received the Scriptures [Jews and Christians] but do not believe in Allah or in the Last Day. They do not forbid what Allah and His Messenger have forbidden. The Christians and Jews do not follow the religion of truth until they submit and pay the poll tax [jizya] and they are humiliated.*

MISSIONS TO WORLD LEADERS

T1561 Mohammed sent letters to the leaders of the countries immediately surrounding Arabia demanding submission to Islam. The leader of Egypt thought enough of the invitation to send Mohammed four slave girls. One of these girls was especially attractive to Mohammed, and she was a Christian. Her name was Mary and, as the reader will remember, she bore him a son.

T1566 The letter was received well by the Christian leader in Rome. He said he knew from the sacred texts that Mohammed was a prophet sent by god and that Christians had been expecting him. He would follow Mohammed except that doing so would get him into political trouble with his Roman superiors. So he sent Mohammed's ambassadors to a Christian bishop instead.

T1567 The bishop also said Mohammed was the one prophesied in the Christian texts and was even mentioned by name. But in the end no one took any action.

T1569 The letter from Mohammed demanding submission to Islam was also sent to the Ethiopian Christian king. The king replied that Mohammed was the one prophesied in the Christian texts and was the prophet of the only god. He sent his son and sixty Ethiopians by boat to Mohammed, and the boat sank.

T1572 When the letter was delivered to the king of the Persians, he tore it up. Mohammed said his kingdom was torn up at that moment.

A SUMMARY OF MOHAMMED'S ARMED EVENTS

1973 In a nine-year period, Mohammed personally attended twenty-seven raids. There were thirty-eight other battles and expeditions. This was a total of sixty-five armed events, not including assassinations and executions, for an average of one every seven weeks over a period of nine years.

M19,4294 *When the Messenger of Allah appointed anyone as leader of an army or detachment, he would especially exhort him to fear Allah and to be good to the Muslims who were with him.*

He would say: Fight in the name of Allah and in the way of Allah. Fight against those who disbelieve in Allah. Make a holy war, do not embezzle the spoils; do not break your pledge; do not mutilate the dead bodies; and do not kill the children.

When you meet your enemies who are polytheists, invite them to three courses of action. If they respond to any one of these, you also accept it and withhold yourself from doing them any harm. Invite them to accept Islam; if they respond to you, accept it from them and desist from fighting against them. Then invite them to migrate from their lands to the land of Islam and inform them that, if they do so, they shall have all the privileges and obligations of the Muslims. If they refuse to migrate, tell them that they will have the status of Bedouin Muslims and will be subjected to the Commands of Allah like other Muslims, but they will not get any share from the spoils of war except when they actually fight with the Muslims against the disbelievers.

If they refuse to accept Islam, demand from them the jizya [the tax of submission]. If they agree to pay, accept it from them and hold off your hands. If they refuse to pay the tax, seek Allah's help and fight them. When you lay siege to a fort and the besieged appeal to you for protection in the name of Allah and His Prophet, do not accord to them the guarantee of Allah and His Prophet, but accord to them your own guarantee and the guarantee of your companions for it is a lesser sin that the security given by you or your companions be disregarded than that the security granted in the name of Allah and His Prophet be violated.

When you besiege a fort and the besieged want you to let them out in accordance with Allah's Command, do not let them come out in accordance with His Command, but do so at your own command for you do not know whether or not you will be able to carry out Allah's behest with regard to them.

NIGHT RAID

B4,52,73 *Allah's Apostle said, "Know that Paradise is under the shades of swords."*

1974 Mohammed sent Ghalib on a night cavalry raid on an Arab tribe. Near the village, he and his men captured one of the tribe's leaders who said he was now a Muslim. He was told that, if he was a Muslim, then one night tied up would do him no harm. They bound him and left him guarded by a black man, who was ordered to kill him if he tried to alert the rest of the tribe.

> B4,52,256 *As-Sab Bin Jaththama said, "The Prophet passed by me at a place called Al-Abwa or Waddan and was asked whether it was permissible to attack the pagan warriors at night with the probability of exposing their women and children to danger."*
>
> *The Prophet replied, "The women and children are from pagans." I also heard the Prophet saying, "The institution of Hima [reserved pasture land] is invalid except for Allah and His Apostle."*

1974 The cavalry got to the tribal area at night. One of them went to scout and lay down on a hill overlooking the village. A villager saw a dark shape on the hill and thought the scout might be a dog. He shot the "shape" twice with arrows, but the scout did not move; so the man figured the shape was not something that was alive.

1974 When the tribe had herded in their cattle, milked them, and gone to bed, they were attacked by the jihadists who cried out, "Slay, slay." Some of the tribe were killed, and their cattle were driven off. The cries of the injured attracted the attention of the other tribe members, and the Muslims fled with the cattle. As they were pursued, the thieves went down through a dry gulch, but soon thereafter a flood came down the gulch and prevented pursuit by the injured tribe. The Muslims took the stolen cattle to Mohammed.

THE RAID AGAINST THE JUDHAM

1976 Mohammed sent an envoy to a Byzantine chief. On the way home, the envoy was raided and lost all his goods to the tribe of Judham. The envoy appealed to a neighboring tribe who were under treaty with Mohammed. They attacked the Judham and recovered the stolen goods.

> B4,52,196 *Mohammed said, "I have been directed to fight the non-Muslim until every one of them admits, 'There is only one god and that is Allah.' Whoever says, 'There is only one god and that is Allah,' his body and possessions will be protected by me except for violations of Islamic law, in which case his fate is with Allah, to be punished or forgiven as He sees fit."*

1977 When the envoy returned to Mohammed and told the story, Mohammed sent out Zayd with armed men for vengeance against the thieves. The men attacked what they thought was the enemy clan, killing five men and stealing one hundred women and children as well as their cattle.

1978 When the chief of the clan found out what had happened, he saddled his camel and took a letter in the form of a treaty to Mohammed. The

Muslim army had attacked the wrong clan; this clan had a treaty with Mohammed. So Mohammed had Ali go out and meet the victorious armed band, and they returned the women, children, and cattle to the clan. The clan forgave them the five dead.

ZAYD'S RAID

> B4,52,259 *Allah's Apostle sent us on a mission and said, "If you find so-and-so and so-and-so, burn both of them with fire."*
>
> *When we intended to depart, Allah's Apostle said, "I have ordered you to burn so-and-so and so-and-so, and it is none but Allah Who punishes with fire, so, if you find them, just kill them."*

1980 The same commander, Zayd, was attacked by a tribe and, besides losing the fight, was personally wounded. While healing from his wounds, he swore not to have sex until he had avenged his pride. So when he was healed he set out to settle the score. This time he was more successful and triumphed over the enemy. One of the leader's wives was an old woman; her legs were tied to two camels, and she was torn apart. Her daughter was taken back to Medina as a pleasure slave for one of Mohammed's men, who in turn gave her to another man. They produced a son who grew up to become a leading legal scholar.

T1559 Another woman had the misfortune to be the fairest of the Arabs. She became the slave of Salama, who brought her back to Medina. Mohammed said, "Salama, how excellent was the father who begot you! Give me the woman." Salama replied, "Messenger of Allah, I have not yet stripped her clothing. She is yours." Mohammed sent her to Mecca as a slave to trade for some captured Muslims.

ANOTHER KILLING OF JEWS

> B4,52,176 *Allah's Apostle said, "Muslims will fight with the Jews till some of them will hide behind stones. The stones will betray them saying, 'O Abdullah [slave of Allah]! There is a Jew hiding behind me; so kill him.'"*

1981 One of the Jews of Khaybar was trying to work with another Arab tribe to resist the jihad of Islam. Word got back to Mohammed. This was before Khaybar was conquered by Mohammed, and it took some strategy to kill the man. Mohammed sent an agent with several other Muslims who went to the Jew as friends. They treated him well and said Mohammed wished to give him an appointment and honor him.

1981 The Muslims and a company of Jews left for Medina but, about six miles outside Khaybar, the Jew they were trying to assassinate got suspicious and started to turn back. One of the Arabs rushed him with a sword and cut off his leg. The Jew returned the blow with a stick he had in his hand and wounded the attacker in the head. The other Muslims fell upon the other Jews and killed them, except for one who managed to escape.

1981 When they got back to Mohammed, he spit on the head wound and the wound did not fester or cause any pain.

ANOTHER ENEMY OF ALLAH KILLED

1982 Another Arab leader was trying to get men together to resist the onslaught of Mohammed. So Mohammed chose one of his best men to assassinate him. The assassin asked Mohammed how he would recognize the leader. Mohammed said, "He looks like Satan. When you see him you will shudder."

1982 The assassin put his sword on and headed to the town where the leader was supposed to be. He came upon a man with several women. He felt a shudder and advanced toward the man while repeating prayers. The leader asked him who he was. The assassin said, "An Arab who has heard of you and the gathering of force to oppose Mohammed." The leader said he was indeed the man. The assassin walked with him a short distance and then killed him with his sword and fled with the women.

1982 The assassin returned to Mohammed. Mohammed looked at him and said, "The aim is accomplished." The assassin replied, "I have killed him, O Apostle." He replied, "You are right." Then Mohammed took him into the house and gave him a stick and told him to keep it by him. When the assassin went into Medina, people asked him about the stick but he didn't know what it meant. So he went back to Mohammed and asked about the meaning of the stick. Mohammed told him, "It is a sign between you and me on the day of resurrection. There are a few men who will be carrying sticks then."

1982 So the assassin fastened it to his sword and carried it every day. When he was buried, it was put into the grave with him.

THE RAID OF THE DOWRY

1989 A Muslim agreed to marry a woman and pay a high dowry price. He went to Mohammed for help with the dowry and told him the price. Mohammed said, "If you could just pick up money from the ground you could not have offered a higher price."

1990 A few days later there was news of a man who was daring to oppose Mohammed. The man was about a day's ride away. So the husband-to-be was put in charge of a small raiding party to see about the man and the degree of his threat. Mohammed gave them a very old and weak camel and the men set off.

1990 They arrived at the village of the suspected Arab at about sunset. The bridegroom went down to one end of the village, and his men went to the other. When the men heard, "Allah Akbar," they were to charge.

1990 A shepherd from the village had gone out earlier and not returned, so the villagers became worried. The chief took his sword and went out to look for the shepherd. His companions begged him not to go out alone, but he was not afraid and went out.

1990 When the chief came upon him, the Muslim shot him through the heart with an arrow and he died without a word. The Muslim cut off his head and charged into the camp yelling, "Allah Akbar," and his soldiers did the same. Everyone in the camp fled. The Muslims drove off the entire herd of camels and sheep. When the leader took the livestock and the head back to Mohammed, he was given thirteen camels. The price of the camels paid the dowry and he was married.

T1609 There were four women captured as slaves, and one was very beautiful. When Mohammed heard about her he said, "Give her to me." He then gave her to a jihadist as a favor.

ORDERS FOR A RAID

1992 Abdullah was to be a leader of a raid and presented himself for orders. He was wearing a black turban, and Mohammed had him take it off and showed him how to wear it so that a small amount of the cloth hung down in the back. Mohammed said, "That is neater and better." He then gave Abdullah the banner for the troops and said, "Take the banner. Fight everyone in the way of Allah (jihad) and kill those who disbelieve in Allah. Do not cheat about the spoils of war. Do not mutilate or kill children. This is Allah's law and my practice."

THE DEATH OF A POETESS

1996 There was a poetess who wrote a poem against Islam. Mohammed said, "Who will rid me of Marwan's daughter?" One of his followers heard him and on that very night he went to the woman's home to kill her.

M239 The assassin, a blind man, was able to do the work in the dark as the woman slept. Her babe lay on her breast while her other children slept in the room. The stealthy assassin removed the child and drove the knife into her with such force that he pinned her to the bed.

1996 In the morning he went to Mohammed and told him. Mohammed said, "You have helped Allah and his apostle." When asked about the consequences, Mohammed said, "Two goats won't butt their heads together over this."

M239 Mohammed turned to the people in the mosque and said, "If you wish to see a man who has assisted Allah and his prophet, look here." Omar cried, "What, the blind Omeir!" "No," said Mohammed, "call him Omeir the Seeing."

1996 The mother, Marwan, had five sons and the assassin went to the sons and said, "I killed Bint Marwan, O sons. Withstand me if you can; don't keep me waiting." Islam became powerful that day, and many became Muslims when they saw the power of Islam.

MOHAMMED'S DEATH

I1000 One night Aisha complained of a headache, but Mohammed also had a headache and he said, "No, Aisha, O my head. Would it distress you if you were to die before me so that I might wrap you in your shroud and pray over you?" Aisha said, "I think that, if you did that, after you returned to the house you would simply spend the night with one of your other wives." But the pain became worse and he took his final illness in the house of Aisha.

I1006 Mohammed was weakened and in a great deal of pain. Later he died with his head in Aisha's lap.

T1834 His final words were, "There should not be two religions in Arabia" (*i.e.*, no Jews, no Christians).

Mohammed had established the ideal Islamic pattern of religious tolerance. Islam was to be dominant. All other religions had to submit to Islam.

T1831 Mohammed was buried beneath his bed. The bed was removed and a grave was dug where the bed had stood.

I1017 Abu Bakr was elected caliph to rule over Islam after Mohammed's death.

This marks the end of Ishaq's *Sirat Rasul Allah*, translated by A. Guillaume as *The Life of Mohammed*.

MOHAMMED, THE PERSON

CHAPTER 25

4.170 People! The Messenger has come to you with truth from your Lord. If you believe, it will be better for you. But if you do not believe, know that all that is in the heavens and earth belongs to Allah. Allah is all-knowing and wise!

There are many historical documents that give us a very good picture of what Mohammed looked like and what his traits were. One of the primary foundation texts, the Hadith of Bukhari, devotes a chapter to the subject.

He was slightly above average in height with black hair and black eyes. His complexion is described as white in many different Traditions (Hadith). His complexion was light enough that he could be red in the face when he was angry. The Traditions mention his anger many times. He was a fast walker and leaned forward as he walked.

When he met people he looked them straight in the eye and never was the first to break the gaze. When he shook hands he never withdrew his hand first.

He was a simple man when it came to possessions and money. He repaired his own sandals and clothes. Mohammed would help around the house with the work. He thought it was wasteful to spend money on real estate, and that even included the mosque. He strongly preferred rustic plainness to fanciness. Yet given all of that, he dyed his hair, wore scents, and used eye makeup.

His clothing was plain. There were times he put on fancy clothes only to reject them later as being distracting. He ate with his fingers and would lick them clean before washing them.

He said that his desires were women, scents, and food. His fondness for women is surely measured by his marriage to about ten women, ranging in ages from 6 years to more than 40. Also, upon seeing his adopted son's wife's figure, he convinced his son to divorce her and then married his former daughter-in-law. On the other hand he was faithful to his first wife, Khadija, who was independently wealthy.

His house abutted the mosque and was a mud brick structure. Each wife had her own room, which was separated from the other rooms by a simple wall of palm-branches daubed with mud. The door was simply a cloth curtain and one could reach up and touch the ceiling.

He was very modest about sex, and we can tell from one hadith that he had sex with his robes on. He also fondled his wives with their clothes on; however, he would urinate by simply turning his back.

As his power grew, he became more regal and demanding about how he was dealt with. Visitors had to talk in a subdued voice. His word was unquestioned law.

He is called illiterate and his illiteracy is given as proof that he must have been inspired by Allah. This is a strange argument since other illiterate blind people have made their living by composing and reciting poetry and sagas. Homer comes to mind. There is a hadith that has Mohammed call for paper and pen to write. It seems almost impossible that he ran a business as a caravan trader to Syria without being able to read numbers and highly improbable that he was totally illiterate. In either case, his secretaries recorded the written Koran.

He never turned down an invitation to eat. He was democratic and would accept an offer to visit or eat with the lowest person. If a guest ate at his house, it was time to leave when the meal was over. It was easy to gain entry to see him. As Islam grew richer, it became the custom to bring him a present.

To a Muslim, he was the best of friends. He was kind, self-denying, generous, patient, and affectionate. He was the best of friends and the worst of enemies. If an enemy became a Muslim, then all was forgiven; but until he became a Muslim Mohammed never forgot a slight or criticism.

He was affectionate with children, stopping to talk to them and play with them. However, this is a contradictory element of the Sira: few references are made to Mohammed as a father. His relationship with his daughter Fatima is about the only mention of his children, and it was not always harmonious and relaxed. The day after his death she accosted the new ruler, Abu Bakr, for money from Mohammed's estate and was refused because he had left her nothing. She died upset with this state of affairs.

To his enemies, he was cruel. He tortured a Jewish chief to get his money. He prayed during of the torture of a captured black slave of the enemy. He had his enemies' bodies thrown into a well as he stood over them in triumph. He sanctioned forced sex with the women of the defeated, even in front of their husbands. He was elated at the murder of his enemies and cheered when their heads were brought to him. He and his wife watched for hours as eight hundred Jews, who had surrendered, were butchered in cold blood and buried in the marketplace. He exiled two tribes of Jews from Medina and confiscated their wealth.

The term *slave* is a positive one in Islam. Mohammed referred to himself and Muslims as the slaves of Allah. Mohammed's second convert was a slave.

Mohammed himself was involved in every single aspect of slavery. He had non-believing men killed so their women and children could be made slaves[1]. He gave slaves away for gifts[2]. He owned many slaves, some of them black[3]. He passed around slaves for the purpose of sex to his companions, men who were his chief lieutenants[4]. He stood by while others beat slaves[5]. He shared the pleasure of forced sex with women slaves after conquest[6]. He captured slaves and wholesaled them to raise money for jihad[7]. One of his favorite sexual partners was a slave, who bore him a son[8]. He got slaves as gifts from other rulers[9]. The very pulpit he preached from was made by a slave[10]. He ate food prepared by slaves[11]. He was treated medically by a slave[12]. He had a slave tailor[13]. He declared that a slave who ran away from his master would not have his prayers answered[14]. And he approved an owner's having sex with his slaves[15].

Mohammed had two sets of ethics—one for Muslims and the other for non-Muslims. How he treated people depended on which they were. The entire life of Mohammed is divided into the time before he started calling himself a prophet and the time after he became a prophet. As a businessman he showed the same face to all men. After he became a prophet, he showed two faces, one to Muslims and another to non-Muslims. Non-Muslims were cursed, condemned, called names, tortured, killed, exiled,

1. A. Guillaume, *The Life of Muhammad* (London: Oxford University Press, 1982), 466.
2. Ibid., p. 499.
3. Ibid., p. 516.
4. Ibid., p. 593.
5. Ibid., p. 295.
6. Ibid., p. 496.
7. Ibid., p. 466.
8. William Muir, *The Life of Mohammed* (AMS Press, 1975), 425.
9. Ibid., p. 425.
10. Bukhari, Hadith, Volume 1, Book 8, Number 440.
11. Ibid., Volume 3, Book 34, Number 295.
12. Ibid., Volume 3, Book 36, Number 481.
13. Ibid., Volume 7, Book 65, Number 344.
14. Muslim, Hadith, Book 001, Number 0131.
15. Ibid., Book 008, Number 3383.

raped, ethnically cleansed, and despised. But to Muslims he was kind, almost a father figure, an elder brother.

He always took the offensive, when possible. Islam always drew first blood. Mohammed was totally confident—a highly desirable quality for a military man.

THE FOUR RIGHTLY GUIDED CALIPHS

CHAPTER 26

*24.56 Observe your prayers, pay the poor tax, and obey
the Messenger so that you may receive mercy. Never think
that the unbelievers can thwart Allah's plan on earth.
Their destination will be the Fire, a wretched home.*

Immediately after Mohammed's death, Islam had a problem. The prophet was dead, and there would never be another prophet. Allah was never going to communicate with humanity again, but Mohammed, the general and supreme leader, had to be replaced immediately. Before the body got cold, there were political meetings. The Helpers of Medina had their own meeting to select a leader, but the Immigrants had another idea. There must be only one leader, not one for the Helpers and one for the Immigrants, and that leader had to be from the elite tribe, the Quraysh, the Meccan tribe of Immigrants. The Quraysh were to be the supreme tribe of all peoples of the world for all time. All men were inferior to the Quraysh.

ABU BAKR

The first caliph (*khalifa,* successor) was chosen, Abu Bakr. To this day, a caliph is the absolute leader of the state and the religion; there is no concept of separation of church and state in Islam. The leading men chose Abu Bakr and the rest of the common folk approved. He was the first of four caliphs who were called the "rightly guided" because they had been companions of Mohammed and their rule was considered an extension of the prophet's.

Since the fruit does not fall far from the tree, it is instructive to see how the works of the rightly guided caliphs turned out.

As soon as word was out that Mohammed was dead, most of the Muslims decided they wanted to leave Islam, its control, and the payment of taxes. To leave Islam was apostasy, and apostasy was (and still is) a capital offense.

> B9,83,17 *Mohammed said, "The blood of a Muslim who con-
> fesses that none has the right to be worshipped but Allah and that
> I am His Apostle cannot be shed except in three cases: In equity*

*for murder, a married person who commits illegal sexual inter-
course, and the one who reverts from Islam [apostate] and leaves
the Muslims."*

Abu Bakr took care of the apostate problem by killing all who wanted
to leave Islam during what were called the apostasy wars; thousands were
killed. After that, Arabia was content with Islam.

> B9,84,59 *When the Prophet died and Abu Bakr became his suc-
> cessor, some of the Arabs reverted to disbelief. Umar said, "O Abu
> Bakr! How can you fight these people although Allah's Apostle
> said, 'I have been ordered to fight the people till they say: "None
> has the right to be worshipped but Allah" '?"*
>
> *Abu Bakr said, "By Allah! I will fight whoever differentiates
> between prayers and zakat [tax] as zakat is to be taken from
> property according to Allah's Orders. By Allah! If they refused to
> pay me even a baby goat they used to pay to Allah's Apostle, I
> would fight with them for withholding it."*

Not resting on his laurels, Abu Bakr launched an attack upon the Byzantine Empire by attacking Iraq. This was very successful and the jihad
continued until his death. He reigned for four years and made arrange-
ments for Umar to succeed him.

UMAR

Umar took over and conquered Egypt, Syria, and Persia. He set up the
administration of the empire and its system of government. One of his
most famous documents was the treaty of Umar for the dhimmitude of
the Christians. This is a document of eternal second-class citizenship for
Christians and Jews as dhimmis.

One of the problems he had to solve was how to integrate the jihadists
into the conquered community. The jihadists lived in separate cities and
quarters. He stopped the division of the spoils of war to the jihadists and
substituted a state payment. He created a permanent standing army with
a salary.

> B4,53,380 *Umar drove all the non-Muslims from Arabia. After
> Mohammed conquered Khaybar, he considered expelling the Jews
> from the land of Allah, Mohammed, and the Muslims. However,
> the Jews asked Mohammed if they could stay in exchange for their
> servitude and half of each harvest. Mohammed said, "You may
> stay on those terms as long as it pleases us." The Jews remained
> until Caliph Umar drove them from Arabia.*

Umar was a giant of a man, who lived very simply and was more feared than loved. He was harsh with others and himself. For instance, he beat his son to death for drunkenness.

After setting up the general administrative model of Islam, and after ten years of rule, he was assassinated. Ironically, his assassin was a slave he had captured who had once been a Persian general. On his death bed Umar chose six Quraysh to select the next caliph.

> B4,53,388 *Juwairiya said to Umar, "O Caliph, give us your advice."*
>
> *Umar said, "You should continue the arrangement made by Mohammed regarding the dhimmis because the taxes they pay fund your children's future."*

UTHMAN

The six men selected Uthman. Ali, Mohammed's son-in-law, joined the opposition ranks.

There was a new problem. The violent expansion of Islam had slowed down and the newly conquered lands were not as rich as earlier conquests. The empire based upon theft had new problems—money problems.

Umar had replaced the old spoils-of-war system with a stipend. All the spoils and taxes went back to the caliph, and he doled out the money. That worked well as long as there was a flood of money, but now the soldiers wanted more. Islam turned out to be just like all central governments: the money stayed under the control of the caliph and the central government lived very well. Discontent flourished and malcontents made their way from the conquered areas to Medina to besiege Uthman.

When the malcontents heard that reinforcements would arrive in support of Uthman, they attacked and killed him. Umar had been killed by a non-Muslim, but Uthman was killed by Muslims, one of them a son of Abu Bakr. His body was put on a garbage dump and dogs ate part of the body; it was a scandal.

ALI

Ali, the man whom some thought should have been the first caliph, became the next one.

He continued the persecution of those who left Islam, apostates.

> B4,52,260 *Ali burnt some people and this news reached Ibn Abbas, who said, "Had I been in his place, I would not have burnt them as the Prophet said, 'Don't punish anybody with Allah's*

Punishment.' No doubt, I would have killed them for the Prophet said, 'If a Muslim discards his religion, kill him.' "

There were malcontents who went to Mecca and made an alliance with Aisha against Ali. Aisha watched from a camel as Ali won a battle. After the battle, she was sent back to Mecca and placed in seclusion, or house arrest.

But the civil war was not over. The governor of Syria would not recognize Ali as caliph and demanded that the killers of his relative, Uthman, be turned over to him for vengeance. Ali, who had been on friendly terms with the killers, refused, so he and the governor went to battle. The battle went against the governor, but he made the suggestion that arbitration be used to settle the dispute. This seemed reasonable to Ali and he agreed, but the decision went against Ali in two ways: first, because the arbitrators ruled against him; second, because many of his supporters left him since they believed he should have fought the governor until Allah's will was satisfied. Ultimately, his supporters rebelled against him.

Ali decided to attack his rebels first and was victorious, but these were very pious men and there was an outcry of indignation at their deaths. Others criticized Ali for rejecting the decision in the first place. When Ali then tried to attack the Syrian governor, he could not get enough support for an army.

A second caliph committee met to choose a new caliph. While this was going on, Ali was assassinated by one of the relatives of the rebel group. Ali's son was persuaded not to try to be caliph and the governor of Syria became the next supreme ruler.

The governor, now caliph, had a very successful rule. Under his rule, the main branch of Islam, the Sunni, became established.

When his son became the caliph, the old factions emerged. The new caliph demanded that three key members of the opposition come and pay him homage. Only one of them did, and Ali's son, Al Husayn, became head of an armed resistance. The caliph slew them all in battle, including Al Husayn, the grandson of Mohammed. He became a martyr whose death is remembered each year by the Shia Muslims.

So in a brief summary:

Abu Bakr—slaughtered thousands of apostates.

Umar—assassinated by a slave he had captured.

Uthman—assassinated by Muslims.

Ali—assassinated by Muslims.

Al Husayn (Ali's son)—killed by Muslims in battle.

The die was cast for the future of Islam.

COMMENTS

CHAPTER 29

*3.53 Our Lord! We believe in what Thou hast
revealed, and we follow the Apostle; then write
us down among those who bear witness.*

DUAL ETHICS

Islam's success, measured by membership, came when Mohammed
entered the political realm after he moved to Medina. His politics were
based upon a dualistic ethical system with one set of ethics for Muslims
and another set of ethics for non-Muslims. An example of this duality is
that a Muslim should not lie to another Muslim, but on several occasions
Mohammed gave permission to lie to non-Muslims to advance the cause
of Allah.

This dual ethical system was necessary to implement jihad, and it re-
mains in place today. Dual ethics create an "other" that can be treated
differently from a Muslim. Dual ethics are necessary to create the prime
duality of the Islamic world-view:

dar al Islam, land of submission

dar al harb, land of war

What little we know about Mohammed's early life shows that he was
a friend to all and treated all people as he wanted to be treated. But when
he ceased to be a businessman and became a prophet, his world-view and
his ethics changed. Humanity became divided into two groups—Muslim
and non-Muslim, and he treated these two groups differently. Mohammed's reactions to each person depended upon whether that person was
a Muslim.

Mohammed's political view was profoundly and fundamentally dualistic. Unity of humanity would come only when the whole world submitted
to Islam.

A person following in the footsteps of Mohammed believes only Muslims are protected by Islam. A non-Muslim does not have to be granted the
usual considerations of morality such as equality, brotherhood, honesty, and
compassion. From the examples we see in Mohammed's life, non-Muslims

can be mocked, cursed, maligned, threatened, tortured, killed, robbed, assassinated, or enslaved to advance the cause of Islam.

Good and evil are defined in the Trilogy. If an action against a non-Muslim advances Islam, then the action is good. Anything that resists Islam is evil.

JIHAD

Duality of ethics was the basis for Mohammed's greatest single innovation—jihad. Jihad is dual ethics with sacred violence. The key religious element of the dual ethics is that Allah sanctifies violence for complete domination. The non-Muslims must submit to Islam.

Jihad is usually called "holy war" but this is far too narrow a view. Jihad means struggle or effort and is a process that is shown by the life of Mohammed, the perfect jihadist. In Mecca, Mohammed demonstrated the initial practice of jihad when Islam was weak: persuasion and conversion. When he moved to Medina, he demonstrated how jihad worked when Islam was strong: using immigration against inhabitants, creating political power by struggling against the host, dominating other religions, using violence, and establishing a government.

THE JIHAD OF MECCA

From the standpoint of war, jihad did not begin until Mohammed's first killing attack in Medina. But its roots go back to Mecca when Mohammed cursed the ancient native Arabic gods. Jihad is a force that still manifests itself according to circumstances. The violence may go no further than aggressive arguments, beatings, put-downs, hostility, insults, or threats, but it is always based upon an ethical system of duality that started in Mecca.

In Mecca, Mohammed promised his critics' slaughter. When heated arguments broke out between the Meccans and Muslims, it was a Muslim who picked up a weapon and drew blood. It was a Muslim, Umar, who violently protested over a poem. Mohammed was in Mecca when he signed a blood oath with the Muslims of Medina.

The root of the violence of Medina was the peace of Mecca. A peace that demanded submission.

THE SUPREME MASTER OF COMPLETE WAR

Mohammed was the supreme master of complete war and has had no equal to this day. His understanding of the use of force was sophisticated

163

and subtle. Physical violence was only a small part of his understanding of war. That is why comparisons make him superior to military men such as Julius Caesar. Other military geniuses established empires, but none of them had a process for war and empire that lasted for fourteen-hundred years and is still going strong.

Mohammed's profound insight was not just the waging of physical war but war of the mind, emotions, culture, politics, and religion. There is no aspect of being human that Mohammed did not use for war. Money, salvation, sex, culture, religion, destiny, family, immigration, legal codes, government, power, deceit, racial pride, tribalism, community, fear, propaganda, diplomacy, spy-craft, philosophy, ethics, and psychology were all used for jihad. Jihad was not holy war but complete and total civilizational war.

ISLAMIZATION OF A CULTURE

The Sira gives a dynamic picture of how Islam enters a culture. When Mohammed started preaching in Mecca, there was no animosity. Islam was portrayed as a logical continuation of the native Arabic religions. Then Islam claimed to be a "brother religion" to Judaism. Next it became not just a better religion but the best, and all of the other religions were wrong. Islam was publicly confrontational, attacking every aspect of the host culture. Hostility developed between Islam and the Meccan culture of religious tolerance. The Meccans tried to placate the Muslims, but there could be no compromise. Islam turned increasingly to violence that culminated in a treaty of war with new allies in Medina.

When the Muslims immigrated to Medina, the Immigrants were peaceful. But when the Jews said that Mohammed was not a prophet in the Jewish tradition, Islam became hostile. Islam was the better religion; and if logic did not show that, then forceful arguments would. Up to this point, the process of Islam in Medina was the same as in Mecca.

The Immigrants were very poor and there was little growth of the religion. In Medina Mohammed found a way to obtain money and settle old scores with the Meccans who had never submitted to Islam. The solution was political—jihad against the Meccans, the Jews, and their neighbors. By jihad, political Islam conquered all of Arabia in nine years.

MOHAMMED AND THE JEWS

The relationship between Mohammed and the Jews takes up a very large part of the Sira. In Mecca, Mohammed's relationship with them was religious. Mohammed identified Allah with Jehovah. (Mohammed never explained who Allah was. He did not have to. Allah, the moon god, was chief of the many gods in the Kabah. The Quraysh tribe swore all oaths by Allah long before Mohammed did.) The Koran adopted the Jewish stories about Moses, Adam, and others to make the point that Allah would punish those who didn't obey His prophets.

He took this stance when he was in Mecca where there were very few Jews. In contrast, Medina was about half Jewish. Their leaders were weak debaters but, even so, they let Mohammed know he was not a Jewish prophet. The tone of Mohammed and the Koran then changed regarding Jews. The theological ground was laid for their destruction.

The first Jewish tribe had the choice of conversion or exile and losing their possessions. The second tribe had the same choice. But the third tribe of Medina had the choice of conversion or death. The Jews of Khaybar had the choice of conversion or dhimmitude, a permanent second-class legal status.

The Jews were never able to make real alliances against Islam. Each tribe of Jews stood alone in its fight against Islam and each lost.

DHIMMIS

The relationship between Islam on the one hand and Christians and Jews on the other was formed by Mohammed. The relationship is the dhimmi status, or dhimmitude, as established at Khaybar after the Jews were crushed. A dhimmi is a Jew or Christian who agrees to be a second-class citizen politically, culturally, and religiously. He sacrifices all civil rights and pays a special tax of humiliation. Indeed, the cash flow of the empire of Islam was based upon this special tax, the *jizya*.

Other conquerors have used war to steal money by taxation, but what crippled the Jews was that Mohammed took Jehovah and the Torah from them and made them submit to Islam. Then Christ became just another prophet and he made the Christians submit to Islam. Mohammed's deathbed directive allowed no Jews or Christians in Arabia. There has been religious apartheid in Arabia ever since.

RAPE?

Muslims had sex with the captive women after battles. This is reported in the Sira and many times in the Hadith and approved in the Koran.

But is this rape? In jihad, it is not rape to have forced sex with a woman, even if she is married, as long as she is a non-Muslim captive or slave. A

Muslim does not commit rape if the woman is a non-Muslim, only if she is a Muslim. Again Islam presents dual ethics.

Forced sex with women after their protectors have been killed is supreme domination. It also humiliates male relatives and husbands who were not killed. If it is followed by capture and relocation to the captor's environment, it usually results in a totally compliant woman who has been forced to submit. Forced sex with women was an ancient method of war because it worked. If the woman's children were raised as Muslims, the domination ensured cultural and familial annihilation. Still in practice today, forced sex is far more than rape; it is a method of war, a tactical strike. Naturally, it is not a crime because it is jihad. It is not a sin because it is sanctioned in the Trilogy of the Koran, the Sira, and the Hadith.

SLAVERY

Mohammed captured slaves, sold slaves, bought slaves, freed slaves, tortured slaves, had sex with slaves, gave slaves as gifts of pleasure, received slaves as gifts, and used slaves for work. The Sira is exquisitely clear on the issue of slavery.

In Islam, slavery is a blessing. Either the slave or his family will one day convert to Islam in order to be freed, thereby creating new Muslims.

REAL ISLAM AND DUALISTIC LOGIC

The doctrine of Islam developed in Mecca contradicts the doctrine developed in Medina. Which is the real Islam? There is not a "real" Islam in the sense of resolving apparent contradictions between the two. Both persuasion-jihad and domination-jihad can be applied as needed.

Mohammed revealed a new logic, the logic of the unresolved contradiction, the logic of duality. Two contradictory statements can both be true if Allah says they are. Therefore, neither is false.

For instance, Mohammed was involved in a violent event every seven weeks for the last nine years of his life, but Mohammed is the prophet of the religion of peace. That is a contradiction but, inside dual logic, both sides of the contradiction are true. Both peace and violence advance Islam; both are good and true. Both are Islam. That is the message of the Sira and the power of Islam.

NAMING

All of the names and terms used by Islam come from the Trilogy. But unbelievers don't use these terms or names.

166

The jihad of Umar burst out of Arabia and crushed the Christian world of Syria, Egypt, and the rest of the Middle East. The Christians recorded it as an Arabic war. When Islam invaded Europe, Europeans called it a Turkish invasion. The jihad against Christian Spain was an invasion by the Moors. The Muslims called these events jihad.

In the early nineteenth century America sent the Navy and Marines to war against the Barbary pirates on the Berber coast in north Africa. For centuries the Islamic Barbary pirates had raided Europe and taken nearly a million white slaves, and their shipping raids in the Mediterranean had taken a great toll. But the Muslims never called their naval raiders "Barbary pirates." They called them *ghazis,* sacred raiders. A raid led by Mohammed against the unbelievers' caravans was called a *ghazwah.* The Muslims were clear that naval raids by the "Barbary pirates" were actually jihad by the army of Mohammed. Naming them "pirates" showed that the unbelievers had no idea about the doctrine and history of Islam.

Look at the news today. The media report an *intifada,* uprising, by the Palestinians against the Israelis. But the terms *intifada, Palestinian,* and *Israeli* are misnomers. The real terms are *jihad* and *infidel,* if we follow the Koran, and the doctrine of political Islam clearly states that jihad is to be waged by all Muslims against all Jews and other "unbelievers." Today is no different from 1400 years ago in Islam.

9/11 is recorded in the West as a terrorist attack by terrorists. Mohammed Atta, the leader of the 9/11 attack, was a pious Muslim. He left a letter clearly stating his intentions: 9/11 was pure jihad. An attack is a single event, but jihad is a 1400-year continuous process. Therefore, a terrorist attack is not the same as jihad. *Terrorism* does not have the same meaning as *jihad.*

What do the terms "moderate Muslim" and "extremist Muslim" actually mean? Only Islam can define what a Muslim is. According to the Trilogy, a Muslim is anyone who follows the pattern (Sunna) of Mohammed. What unbelievers call a moderate, *i.e.* peaceful, Muslim is actually a Muslim behaving as Mohammed did when he lived in Mecca. And an extremist Muslim is really a Medinan Muslim, one following the words and actions of the Prophet when he lived in Medina. Unbelievers call Osama Bin Laden an extremist Muslim, but his actions are carefully based upon those of Mohammed in Medina. Bin Laden, like all jihadists, is a devout Muslim following the Koran of Medina. As far as the Koran is concerned, an extremist Muslim is one who leaves the religion, an apostate.

Unbelievers called them the "Paris riots." Muslims called the burnings and theft the "Great Ramadan Offensive," which connects them to

Mohammed's first jihad in the sacred month of Ramadan. The name "Paris riots" evokes different thoughts, insights, and points of view from the "Great Ramadan Offensive."

The naming of these events by unbelievers does not convey the right meaning. Muslims' names for themselves and their actions connect events and people with Islamic history and doctrine and show a continuing process. Non-Muslim names are temporary, do not connect events, and show no historic process.

The only correct terms are those of Islam. The naming by the unbelievers is wrong because the naming is a projection of Western culture. Correct naming leads to correct thinking.

SUMMARY STATISTICS

Islam is not the worship of Allah. Islam is the worship of Allah by imitating Mohammed. It is interesting to measure by words how much of the foundational doctrine of Islam is devoted to Allah and how much is devoted to Mohammed.

The Koran has 153,000 words; the Hadith of Bukhari has 338,000 words; and the Sira has 408,000 words. So 17% of the doctrine is about Allah (the Koran) and 83% is about Mohammed (Sira and Hadith).

TO THE READER

Take the time to reflect on what you have read and draw your own conclusions. The hope is that you will now read the original of Ishaq's *Sirat Rasul Allah* in A. Guillaume's *The Life of Mohammed.*

FOR MORE INFORMATION

Go to our website:
www.cspipublishing.com

BIBLIOGRAPHY

Watt, W. Montgomery and Bell, Richard. *Introduction to the Quran*. Edinburgh: Edinburgh University Press, 1970.

Robinson, Neal. *Discovering the Koran*. London: SCM Press, 1996.

Arberry, A. J. *The Koran Interpreted*, NY: Touchstone, 1996.

Pickthall, Mohammed M. *The Meaning of the Glorious Koran*. Kuwait: Dar al-Islamiyya.

Warraq, Ibn. *What the Koran Really Says*. Amherst, NY: Prometheus Books, 2002.

Dawood, N. J. *The Koran*, London: Penguin Books, 1999.

Rodwell, J. M. *The Koran*, North Clarendon, VT: Tuttle Publishing, 1994.

Ali, Maulana Muhammad. *Holy Koran*. Columbus, Ohio: Ahmadiyyah Anjuman Ishaat Islam 1998.

Watt, W. Montgomery and M.V. McDonald. *The History of al-Tabari, vol. VI, Muhammad at Mecca*. New York: The State University of New York Press, 1987

McDonald, M.V. and W. Montgomery Watt. *The History of al-Tabari, vol. VII, The Foundation of the Community*. New York: The State University of New York Press, 1987

Michael Fishbone, *The History of al-Tabari VIII The Victory of Islam*. New York: The State University of New York Press, 1987

Poonawala, Ismail K. *The History of al-Tabari, vol. IX, The Last Years of the Prophet*. New York: The State University of New York Press, 1987

Muir, Sir William. *Life of Mohammed*. New York: AMS Press, 1975

Guillaume, A. *The Life of Muhammad*, (Ishaq's—Sirat Rasul Allah). Karachi: Oxford University Press, 1967

The Hadith of Abu Al-Bukhari, *Sahih Bukhari*, and the Hadith of Abu Muslim, *Sahih Muslim*, are best found on the internet. The University of Southern California (http://www.usc.edu/dept/MSA/fundamentals/hadithsunnah/) is one of the best sites.

Printed in the United States
88034LV00006B/179/A

9 780978 552893